SOFTWARE
CONFLICT

SOFTWARE CONFLICT

Essays on the Art and Science of Software Engineering

Robert L. Glass

Computing Trends

YOURDON PRESS
Prentice Hall Building
Englewood Cliffs, New Jersey 07632

Library of Congress Cataloging-in-Publication Data

Glass, Robert L.
    Software conflict : essays on the art and science of software
engineering / Robert L. Glass.
        p.   cm.
    Includes bibliographical references.
    ISBN 0-13-826157-1
    1. Software engineering.   I. Title.
QA76.758.G53   1990
005.1--dc20   89-48115
                                                          CIP

Editorial/production supervision
 and interior design: **Brendan M. Stewart**
Cover and text illustrations: **P. Edward Presson**
Manufacturing buyer: **Kelly Behr**

 ©1991 by Prentice-Hall, Inc.
A Division of Simon & Schuster
Englewood Cliffs, New Jersey 07632

This book can be made available to businesses
and organizations at a special discount when
ordered in large quantities. For more information
contact:

Prentice-Hall, Inc.
Special Sales and Markets
College Division
Englewood Cliffs, N.J. 07632

Printed in the United States of America
10 9 8 7 6 5 4 3 2 1

ISBN 0-13-826157-1

Prentice-Hall International (UK) Limited, *London*
Prentice-Hall of Australia Pty. Limited, *Sydney*
Prentice-Hall Canada Inc., *Toronto*
Prentice-Hall Hispanoamericana, S.A., *Mexico*
Prentice-Hall of India Private Limited, *New Delhi*
Prentice-Hall of Japan, Inc., *Tokyo*
Simon & Schuster Asia Pte. Ltd., *Singapore*
Editora Prentice-Hall do Brasil, Ltda., *Rio de Janeiro*

To Iris,
who helped me grow

The Latest in Weaponry   65

A Postmortem of the Battleground   205

Foreword

Humor is an elusive commodity in most technical books. Yet, when it is present, it makes reading about new ideas fun. That's what I like about Bob Glass's writings. He uses sarcasm and wit to communicate his thoughts on controversies that are currently being debated by the leaders of the software engineering community. He is insightful and entertaining when he states his opinions, some of which are quite controversial. He is humorous and humanistic. A great story teller, he uses revealing anecdotes and parables. Bob Glass is also a teacher who gives us lessons in history, ethics, and philosophy so that he can relate them to his opinions and make his points.

This book is fundamentally about conflict and conflict management. It pits the programmer/software engineer against the manager. It contrasts theory versus practice, discussing stability versus change, talk versus action, and promises versus results. It tries to show us all sides of an argument. It also tries to make us think and reach our own opinions.

The book is also about change and change management. It encourages us to challenge the accepted gospel that change can't happen quickly. It states that there are no panaceas on the horizon in the foreseeable future.

Yet, it asks us to examine "why" the state of the practice of software engineering has to be so different from the state of the art.

The book's main premise is that conflict is healthy when managed properly because it forces professionals to think through their ideas before they rush to implement them. The basic conflict described is the one that exists between theory and practice. Bob takes the side of the practitioner as he goes on to explain that neither side can make progress without contributions to the other.

As a practitioner myself, I can relate well to Bob's opinions and amplifying examples. The many battles that I have fought with academics have been in the same arena. The frustrations that Bob expresses are ones that I have felt myself. The arguments that he poses are ones that I have used myself to win battles, but never the war.

The book is controversial because it tries to explode the myths which permeate the literature. Although I agree with Bob on many points, we still have major areas of disagreement when it comes to technology and its transition. I am an evolutionist, while Bob is a revolutionist. I look for incremental progress, while Bob searches for quicker solutions. Yet, that is the purpose of the book—to make people think and help people change.

As much as I like the book, there are some things wrong with it. First, it is too long. Because Bob has so much to say, he often takes too long to get to his main point. Second, the book is too short. Just when you think that Bob will solve your problem, he stops and forces you to think it through yourself.

Needless to say, I recommend that this book be read. Software managers, software engineers, academics, computer scientists, programmers, and technologists could all benefit from its study. Think about what Bob has to say and ponder its meaning. I am sure that you will find that it has value. Don't take things literally as they appear. Bob is the master of disguise as he says things to get your attention and make you think. If you don't agree with him, all the better. At least now you will have an opinion on some of the topics that will shape the field of software engineering as we will know it in the future.

Donald J. Reifer, President
Reifer Consultants, Inc.

Preface

Conflict and controversy have been too long avoided in computer science and software engineering. These fields are less than a human generation old, with all the growing pains that accompany youth. Yet in the professional literature we tend to see opinions presented as truth and advocacy presented as fact, with nothing acknowledging the tentative nature of some of these facts and much of this truth. Even noted computer scientist David Parnas has labeled much of our computer science truth "folklore," because it has not been experimentally verified.

It isn't that conflict and controversy don't exist in the field. If N computer scientists or software engineers discuss an issue in person, there are often at least N opinions on what is correct or best. (Bill Curtis said it best in his keynote to the 1989 International Conference on Software Engineering— "In a room of 15 designers, if two of them agree that's a majority!")

But in general these conflicts happen in the conference room or the drawing room, not out in the open in the literature. Hiding of the issues sometimes has strange consequences, as when the latent disagreement on the value of formal verification erupted into ugly name calling in 1989 in

Communications of the ACM.[1] (An earlier eruption over that issue about a decade ago, and reported in the introduction to my book, *Software Soliloquies*, was just as turbulent.)

Hiding from the issues is a mistake. Conflict properly confronted can lead to progress. Conflict avoided can lead to polarization, stagnation, and—as we have seen—eruption. This field is too young for people to lock themselves into premature positions and posturing. Major disagreements must be surfaced and aired before open wounds fester.

Often these conflicts take the form of disagreement between theory and practice. In fact, the relative roles of theory and practice in the progress of the discipline are part of the conflict.

In this book, some of these conflicts are examined. Although both sides of issues are presented, the bias in this book favors the practitioner viewpoint. I am a practitioner of 30 years' experience who has dabbled enough in the academic world to be able to say, "My head is in software engineering academics, but my heart lies in its practice."

The conflicts are approached here in a collection of essays, grouped into several major topic areas.

An Overview of the Battleground.

Essays on high-level issues, such as a look at the Parnas Star Wars and the Brooks Silver Bullet papers, are presented. An unusual analysis of the historic relationship between theory and practice is also included.

From the Technical Trenches.

These essays are about software technology. One, for example, looks at the issue of software design, and asks why we continue to focus on the trappings of design (methodologies and representations) rather than the essence of design (cognitive activity).

The Latest in Weaponry.

These essays are about methodology, tools, and languages. One, for example, reviews the literature for quantita-

[1]—The title of the paper that triggered the episode was "Program Verification: The Very Idea," by James H. Fetzer, professor of Philosophy and the Humanities at the University of Minnesota (Duluth). It was published in the September 1988 issue of *Communications*, and it presented a quite negative view of formal verification.

The strongest response to the paper was mustered by a collection of ten formal methods advocates in the March 1989 issue of the same journal, who accused Fetzer of "distortion," "gross misunderstanding," "misrepresentation," "misinformation," and finally of being "ill-informed, irresponsible, and dangerous." Fetzer responded, both guns blazing, saying that his antagonists had a "complete failure to understand the issues," "intellectual deficiencies," "inexcusable intolerance and insufferable self-righteousness," and that they had behaved like "religious zealots and ideological fanatics." He even invited them to "volunteer to accompany . . . missiles on future flights in order to demonstrate . . . program verification" under dynamic circumstances.

There was more similar gunfire in the April issue of *Communications*. It will not be surprising if this issue flames up again in the future.

tive evaluations of the value of CASE tools, 4GL languages, and other productivity approaches, with some surprising results.

From the Command Post.   Some essays on management, marketing, and consulting are presented. Four of them probe the recent hot topic of productivity improvement, providing some judgment on where we have come from and where we might be going.

From the Laboratories.   These essays are on technology transfer of research findings. For example, one is an open letter to computer science professors on the lack of attention to software maintenance in the curriculum, and another cites serious problems in the communication gap between theory and practice.

A Postmortem on the Battleground.   These essays tidy up the way taken. One points to what is lacking in the theoretic approaches to computer science and software engineering and suggests ways of improving those approaches. Another looks at fun in the field, and laments its apparent departure.

And there is an epilog at the end that summarizes the more important ideas of the book in a series of "Pithy Thoughts." (Don't let me catch you sneaking a look at the ending, now!)

The intended audience for this book is anyone who cares about the field of software engineering, be they practitioners, or researchers or academics. That's a tough audience to satisfy. To help reach that audience, I have chosen a mix of writing styles, often serious but also (I hope) often entertaining, and with some use of metaphor and fable, sometimes even writing about real people and places disguised by fictitious names. It is a style I used in a previous book of essays, *Software Soliloquies* (Computing Trends, 1981) and it seemed to work well there.

Now, with that initialization out of the way, I invite you to read on. My hope is that you will have a reaction to what you read here. You may agree with me, or you may disagree, but I hope you won't simply be passive. The conflicts of our field deserve more than just to be swept under a convenient rug.

Robert L. Glass

SOFTWARE
CONFLICT

An Overview of the Battleground

Which Comes First,
Theory or Practice?

Theory: a statement of the principles on which a subject is based.

Practice: action as opposed to theory; to be actively engaged in professional work.

(*Oxford American Dictionary*, 1980.)

The meanings of the words *theory* and *practice* are clear and accepted well enough so that we have little doubt about what people mean when they use them. But what about the temporal relationship between the two notions; that is, which comes first, theory or practice?

For most of us who have spent a decade or more in a school system, the answer is probably automatic: Theory precedes and frames practice. But that automatic answer may be severely flawed, and in that automatic answer may be some profound misunderstandings.

Take, for example, this quotation from Christopher Alexander's *Notes on the Synthesis of Form* (Harvard University Press, 1964):

The airfoil wing section which allows airplanes to fly was invented at a time when it had just been "proved" that no machine heavier than air could fly. Its aerodynamic properties were not understood until some time after it had been in use. Indeed the invention and use of the airfoil made a substantial contribution to the development of aerodynamic theory, rather than vice versa.

According to Alexander, then, practice here preceded theory. Are there more examples of that perhaps surprising idea?

Another such quotation, astounding in its similarity to Alexander's, comes from D. D. Price's "Sealing Wax and String: A Philosophy of the Experimenter's Craft and its Role in the Genesis of High Technology" (*Proceedings of the American Association for the Advancement of Science Annual Meeting*, 1983):

> Thermodynamics owes much more to the steam engine than the steam engine owes to thermodynamics . . . If we look at the usual course of events in the historical record . . . there are very few examples where technology is applied science. Rather it is much more often the case that science is applied technology.

Two instances of practice preceding theory do not prove a case or even establish a trend, of course; but Price suggests that in fact there may be a trend here. Are there more examples?

Herbert A. Simon, in *The Sciences of the Artificial* (The MIT Press, 2nd ed., 1981), says:

> . . . the main route to the development and improvement of time-sharing systems was to build them and see how they behaved. And this is what was done. They were built, modified, and improved in successive stages. Perhaps theory could have anticipated these experiments and made them unnecessary. In fact, it didn't, and I don't know anyone intimately acquainted with these exceedingly complex systems who has very specific ideas as to how it might have done so. To understand them, the systems had to be constructed, and their behavior observed.

Via Simon, the notion that practice precedes theory is beginning to hit closer to home, in our own computing and software worlds. Let us look more at theory and practice in software.

I grew up in the practice of computing and software, and I recall many of the formative events in the field. This notion of practice preceding theory rings true to me. The origins of the computer, of course, go back to the early research labs in institutions scattered across North America and Europe. Yet by the mid 1950s, computing and software were beginning to thrive as professional fields. Practice, if not ahead of theory at the outset, in fact outstripped it as the field evolved. It was not until the 1960s that the academic field of computer science began to emerge. And the theory that came with these early academic pursuits probably did not begin to surface until the late 1960s or early 1970s.

Based on the personal recollections of an old timer in the field, then, the notion that practice precedes theory certainly seems credible. But experience, of course, can be a deceptive teacher. What one person experiences can be far different from what another experiences. Is there some other way to examine this issue?

Thus far I have discussed computing and software as if it were a single discipline, examinable as a whole. But what if, instead, we were to look at some of the constituent elements of that whole? Can we see a pattern of practice and theory emerge from that kind of examination?

How about programming style? Which came first here, practice or theory? Certainly there were a lot of programs written before there were books on programming style. I recall vividly that some of those programs had excellent style, and some did not. I would suggest that style in practice was fairly well developed before a theory of style evolved. (It is interesting to note that an early series of books on style, Ledgard's "Proverbs . . . ," were essentially a codification of good practice).

How about compiler writing? The practice of compiler writing produced compilers for such languages as Fortran, Commercial Translator, FACT, and later COBOL well before there was a well-documented theory of compiler writing. Once again, I would suggest that compiler writing, now a topic at the heart of computer science academically, was fairly well developed in practice before a theory began to emerge.

There are examples of practice leading theory even today. Simulation is a frequently-used tool at the system level to help define requirements and extract a design for complex problems. The topic of simulation, on the other hand, rarely comes up in the computing research world. Recent interest in prototyping is not quite the same thing. (Note that simulation, as used in practice, is the creation of a tentative practical solution in order to establish a theory of the problem. Even here, practice leads theory!)

User interface design, although firmly rooted in theory in its Xerox PARC origins, by now has moved forward more rapidly in (especially micro) computer practice than the theory that supports it.

Design itself is still poorly understood at the theory level. Courses in design frequently focus on methodology and representation, and yet most designers are aware that design is much more complex than simply having a framework for doing it and a way of writing it down. Once again, the practice of design is far ahead of its theory.

And, in fact, the general notion of problem solving, which is what software engineering is really all about, is still in the early stages of theory building (see, for example, Simon's *The Sciences of the Artificial*, referenced earlier) even though the practice of problem solving (like that of design) is centuries old.

In other words, there is example after example of practice preceding theory. Does this surprise you? In spite of my historical perspective, it still surprises me. All of my academic background cries out for the notion that theory builds a framework upon which practice may construct things. If that notion is not true, then perhaps we should examine the implications.

Let us construct a diagram to show the relationship between theory and practice implied by this notion. What follows is my attempt at such a diagram. I believe, in essence, that given a particular discipline, practice comes first and evolves fairly rapidly at the outset; theory starts after there is a practice to formalize, and also evolves rapidly; and then there is a crossover point at which theory moves past practice:

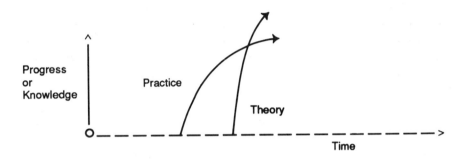

Let us assume for the moment that this relationship holds true. What are its implications?

For one thing, the diagram suggests that in the early stages of a discipline, theory can best progress by examining practice. True, theorists must also be free to formulate new ideas unfettered by past ways of doing things; but nevertheless, there is much to be learned by examining what practice is doing, particularly the best of practice. This is an important thought. For the most part, the development of computing and software theory has not followed the implications of this thought. Few computing theorists are former practitioners. There is little experimental, practice-simulating research in our field. And, except for some of the Empirical Studies of Programmers research, very little study is made of practitioners at work in evolving theory.

This thought suggests that at least the early approach to theory must change. The lore of practical knowledge may be far too rich for theory to ignore it.

Another conclusion that can be drawn from the diagram is that there comes a point at which practice, having been surpassed by theory, must listen to it. The framework that theory can provide in such areas as data bases and data structures, for example, far surpasses the knowledge of most practitioners in those disciplines. Once again, the state of the practice has not reached this point. Just as theory fails to study practice when it is appropriate, practice fails to listen to theory when that becomes appropriate.

In other words, there are fundamental problems in the interactions between theory and practice that the preceding diagram can clarify; and the failure to understand the implications of the diagram is fundamental to the state of the art and practice of computing and software.

Probably the diagram is an oversimplification. In the most accurate of pictures, the progress of practice and theory is more likely an intertwining series of steps, where practice and theory alternately take the lead. But even with that more complex picture, there will be places on this new diagram (zoom-lens snapshots, perhaps) within which the simpler diagram is still valid.

Does practice precede theory? At some levels, and at some points in time, yes it does. Now it is time for both practice and theory to absorb the implications of that fact.

Acknowledgments: The author wishes to thank Iris Vessey and Dale Dowsing for their help in the evolution of these ideas.

"Dangerous and Misleading"
A Look at Software Research
via the Parnas Papers

The controversy over the Star Wars defense system has raged on for some time.

The discussion which follows is *not*, however, about Star Wars. It is about a different view of software which stems from the Star Wars controversy.

You may know that Professor David Parnas, one of the leading computer scientists of our time, withdrew from his role in Star Wars because he believes the software problems of such a system to be insurmountable.

Perhaps you read the Parnas papers which appeared in the *American Scientist*, September–October 1985, and were reprinted in various computing professional journals. Those papers explain why he believes the software portions of the system cannot be built successfully.

But I want to take another, different look at what Parnas said. In his analysis of *why* he believes the system cannot be built, he said some pretty devastating things about the state of the art of software.

This was not an attack on the state of the *practice* of software. Those unfortunately fairly common attacks by some computer scientists say software is "always over budget, behind schedule, and unreliable." You can form your own opinion about those words.

This was, instead, an attack on the state of the *research* of software. Item by item, Parnas explained in his papers why he thought each of the leading research directions of our time will not help Star Wars. And in so doing, he cast a serious shadow on that research. Let us look at some examples of what he said.

You've probably read that dramatic improvements in software productivity are only a new language or a new toolset away. Parnas says no. "We cannot expect [new programming languages] to make . . . a big difference," and "problems with our programming environment have not been a major impediment in our . . . work."

Well, then, what about so-called automatic programming systems, those methodologies that are supposed to make programmers obsolete within a few years? "I believe that the claims that have been made for our automatic programming systems are greatly exaggerated," says Parnas. He goes on to say that "if the input specification is not a description of an algorithm, the result is woefully inefficient . . . there will be no substantial change from our present capability" coming from nonprocedural, automated programming systems.

Perhaps, then, the dramatic gains of artificial intelligence can help us. Here, again, Parnas takes a dim view. There are, Parnas says,

> two quite different definitions of AI in common use today . . .
>
> AI-1: The use of computers to solve problems that previously could be solved only by applying human intelligence.
>
> AI-2: The use of . . . rule-based programming . . . to solve a problem the way humans seem to solve it.

"I have seen some outstanding AI-1 work," says Parnas, but "I cannot identify a body of techniques . . . that is unique to this field." In other words, the learning experience of solving one problem with AI-1 methods does not extend very well to the next problem.

"I find the approaches taken in AI-2 to be dangerous and much of the work misleading . . . program behavior is poorly understood and hard to predict . . . the techniques . . . do not generalize." Parnas's attack here is devastating. Expert systems, he is saying, may not be very trustworthy.

Parnas is also concerned about software reliability. "We do not know how to guarantee the reliability of software," he says. But what then of a proof of correctness, that mathematics-like approach by which a software system can be proven to match its specification? "It is inconceivable to me that one could provide a convincing proof of correctness of even a small portion of [massive] software . . . I do not know what such a proof would mean if I had it." He gives an example: "We have no techniques for proving the correctness of programs in the presence of unknown hardware failures and errors in input data."

Taken in their entirety, the Parnas papers seem to represent a powerful attack on the status of software research. Does Parnas come to grips with this specifically?

"Good software engineering is far from easy," he says. "Those who think that software designs will become easy [via new technologies] and that errors will disappear, have not attacked substantial problems." "I don't expect the next 20 years of research to change [the difficulties of building massive systems]." "Very little of [software research] leads to results that are useful. Many useful results go unnoticed because the good work is buried in the rest."

If indeed software research is off in some questionable directions, what should be done about it? Parnas covers that, also.

> Only people closely familiar with the practical aspects of a problem can judge whether or not they could use the results of a research project . . . . Applied research must be judged by teams that include both successful researchers and experienced systems engineers.

> In other words, researchers who want to produce useful results must involve practitioners in the evaluation process.

Let's stand back, now, and look at the totality of what Parnas has said. It is important to remember, of course, that his remarks were made in the context of massive real-time software systems of the magnitude of Star Wars. But an equally important observation is that many of his objections to the value of current research apply to their use on a broader spectrum of large and perhaps even not-so-large software systems.

Where can we expect productivity breakthroughs in software, the kind that will lead to orders of magnitude improvement?

Not in languages or tools.

Not in automatic programming methodologies.

Not in formal verification of software.

Not in artificial intelligence.

Not, in fact, in any of the currently popular software research endeavors.

It is a discouraging picture for the software practitioner who was hoping for breakthroughs.

It is vital food for thought for the software researcher.

"No Silver Bullet" A Look at Software Research via Fred Brooks

For the past few decades, computing research has held out the promise of dramatic breakthroughs in software productivity. And computing management, desperately wanting to believe the researchers, has reached eagerly for each new development off the researcher's shelf.

The result, for most managers, has been disappointment. To be sure, each new research idea, when put to the test, has produced improvement in productivity. The problem is that the improvement has been marginal enough so managers have come to wonder "why bother?"

Researchers, hearing of this problem, haven't listened very carefully. Instead of exploring why their ideas have not born rich fruit, they tend to respond by saying that the practitioners haven't really adopted their new idea after all, and that no fair tests have been given to computing research advances.

A new viewpoint is emerging on this issue. And it is emerging from the best and brightest minds of the computing field.

First it was David Parnas. In his series of papers attacking the Star Wars project, Parnas also attacked research in the software field, finding it did not—in fact, could not—lead to breakthroughs in practice, and called some of it "dangerous and misleading."

Then that viewpoint was reinforced. Fred Brooks, the author of what is almost undoubtedly the single most important book in the computing field—*The Mythical Man-Month*—and the manager who was in charge of the massive OS/360 project, came out with an echo and a reinforcement and new thoughts on this same issue.

The Brooks position was taken in a paper published in *IEEE Computer* in April 1987. It rapidly became known as the "Silver Bullet" paper because it likened software engineering's fundamental problems to werewolves, which can only be slain by silver bullets, and then went on to establish that there are no silver bullets in the software field.

What did Brooks say? Lots. For one thing, he took the position that the process of building software is hard and always will be. It is hard because of its inherent and necessary complexity: "software entities are more complex . . . than perhaps any other human construct," "software systems have orders-of-magnitude more states than computers do," and "the complexity of software is an essential property" which cannot be wished away by the techniques of other disciplines such as mathematics where simplified models of complex problems are useful problem-solving tools.

Having established that software is hard to build and always will be, Brooks dissected the research directions of software theorists and, just as Parnas did, found them wanting. It is not that the directions are not promising, Brooks said. It is just that the big steps in productivity were already taken by such advances as the first high-order language, and time sharing, and the existence of unified programming environments such as Unix and Interlisp. The advances to be achieved by the current search for silver bullets will lead to considerably less relative advancement. The day of the dramatic breakthrough in software engineering, Brooks suggests, may be behind us.

But Brooks didn't stop there. If we cannot get dramatic productivity improvements through current research directions, then where might we get them? He suggested more mundane yet promising avenues.

1. Buy software rather than building it whenever you can. Package software is more practical in the 1990s than it was in the 1960s, Brooks suggests, not because we know more now about how to build such packages, but because the relative cost of software is now so high (compared to hardware) that businesses are more likely to tailor their functions to a software package than the opposite.
2. Use incremental approaches to building software. Refine requirements for software by prototyping. Develop software incrementally,

so that partial solutions to the problem are available early in the development cycle. If the process of building software is truly hard and always will be, then that process must be attacked by fundamental new approaches.

3. Remember that great software designs come from great designers. Creative software people must be hired and nourished. Brooks suggested such nourishment as (1) identifying top designers as early as possible—the best are not necessarily the most experienced; (2) assign a career mentor to each top prospect; (3) devise and maintain a career development plan and a career file for each; and (4) provide opportunities for these people to interact with and stimulate each other.

So what, in restrospect, have Parnas and Brooks said to us? That software development is a conceptually tough business. That magic solutions are not just around the corner. That it is time for the practitioner to examine evolutionary improvements rather than to wait or hope for revolutionary ones.

Some in the software field find this to be a discouraging picture. They are the ones who still thought breakthroughs were near at hand.

But some of us, those of us crusty enough to think that we are realists, see this as a breath of fresh air. At last, we can focus on something a little more visible than pie in the sky. Now, perhaps, we can get on with the incremental improvements to software productivity that are possible, rather than waiting for the breakthroughs that are not likely to ever come.

Thanks, David Parnas and Fred Brooks, for clearing the way.

A Report from the Best and Brightest

"We do not see any single technological development in the next decade that promises ten-fold improvement in software productivity, reliability, and timeliness."

"Few fields have so large a gap between best current practice and average current practice."

"The big problems are not technical . . . . Today's major problems . . . are . . . management problems."

These are some of the opening shots of a powerfully worded, pertinent report of the "Defense Science Board Task Force on Military Software" released late in the 1980s. The task force, chaired by noted computer scientist Frederick P. Brooks, Jr., and containing what Brooks called "an expert and diligent group" of members, attacked some of the ongoing problems of software head on.

Should the average data processing software person care about a report produced to deal with the problems of *military* software? Given that the report was issued a few years ago, is it still up to date in its viewpoint?

Considering the breadth, depth, and timeliness of this report, my answer is a resounding *yes*. A lot of software dragons are met and slain here; and a lot of others are put in proper perspective. And the people who prepared the report are probably the best and brightest in the business.

I have been mulling over this report and its findings since its release in September 1987. And I have come to see it as perhaps *the* definitive statement of where software "was at" in the late 1980s. I don't agree with all of the conclusions in the report, but I find them tremendously stimulating even when I disagree. I hope you find this summary of the report just as stimulating.

The report is almost breathtaking in the way it tackles both the institutional problems that the military and its contractors have struggled with for years, and the problems of transitioning new technology and management concepts. It indicates major changes in the emphasis the Department of Defense (DOD) should place on software procurement, especially in such longstanding traditional areas as personnel rotation, suggesting that the DOD change, and "structure some officer careers to build a cadre of technical managers with deep technical mastery and broad operational overview." (Presently many military officers change positions about every two years, and are unable to develop mastery of a single technical skill area.)

The report, written to attract the attention of a military body which has ignored many previous such studies, pulls no punches. Written in a powerful style, it contains a series of short and pithy assertions followed by a justification for the assertion and then a recommendation.

For example, regarding past study findings, the report says "Many previous studies have provided an abundance of valid conclusions and detailed recommendations. Most remain unimplemented. If the military software problem is real, it is not perceived as urgent."

Some of the Findings

But how is this report relevant to the average, nonmilitary data processing person? Consider these findings:

- Regarding systems analysis, the report calls requirements-setting "the hardest part" of software development. It sees a built-in and monumental problem in this area, and lays the groundwork for the advocacy of prototyping as a method of solving it:

    The hardest part of the software task is the setting of the exact requirements. There are not even good ways in common use for even stating detailed requirements and trade-off priorities . . . . Misjudgements abound. Most common is the over-rich function, whose bad effects on size and performance become evident only late in the design cycle. Another common error is the mis-imagination of how user interfaces should work. In our view, the difficulty is fundamental. We believe that users cannot . . . accurately describe the operational requirements for a substantial software system without testing by real operators in an operational environment, and iteration on the specification. The systems built today are just too complex for the mind of man to foresee all the ramifications purely by the exercise of the analytic imagination.

- Regarding fourth-generation languages, the report sees profound misunderstandings in this area, and notes that a blend of 3GL and 4GL approaches is warranted:

> The term fourth generation is a misnomer. It has been used to characterize a wide variety of languages which are not descendants of the third generation, general purpose languages. The term encompasses application-specific languages such as database languages and electronic spreadsheets, program generators, non-procedural languages, and even artificial intelligence languages such as Prolog. Each language is designed to be applied to problems in a limited domain. Therefore the fourth generation languages do not compete with Ada (and other general purpose languages).

- Regarding Ada, the report finds expectations out of sync with results. Ada may be a good language, and the report recommends that Ada be given a "serious and determined push," but points out that the problems of software go well beyond the ability of a language to solve them:

> Ada has been overpromised . . . . Support tools are needed for such activities as
> - software documentation writing and formatting;
> - version and configuration control of both software and documentation;
> - maintaining development history in a way that links requirements, design specification, code documentation, source code, compiled code, program reports, code changes, tests, and test run results;
> - debugging; and
> - project schedule and effort management.
>
> As a consequence, non-technical managers of programs are expecting results that no high-level language can by itself deliver.

- Regarding incremental implementation, the reports refers to "professional humility" as the ability to understand our own software development weaknesses. It suggests early release of minimally complete versions of software on the way to full-scale development:

> Experience with confidently specifying and painfully building mammoths has shown it [incremental implementation] to be the simplest, safest and even fastest way to develop a complex software system by building a minimal version, putting it into actual use, and then adding function, enhancing speed, reducing size, etc., according to the priorities that emerge from actual use . . . . Evolutionary development . . .

plays havoc with the customary forms of competitive procurement, however, and they with it. Creativity in acquisition is now needed.

- Regarding off-the-shelf solutions, the report finds the best way to build a software solution is not to build it at all:

> The *cheapest* way to get software is to buy it in the commercial marketplace rather than to build it. The *fastest* way to get software is to buy it in the commercial marketplace rather than to build it. The *surest* way to get software is to buy it in the commercial marketplace rather than to build it.

- Regarding software metrics, the report finds a deep need for measurement of software product quality, and then suggests a workable solution for the problem:

> There are no metrics for source code quality, object code quality, documentation quality, etc. . . . There are techniques for judging the overall quality of complex performances outside the computer field. . . . Even today software quality can be judged by panels of trained judges, just as such panels judge Olympic diving, skating and acrobatic performances."

Some of the Recommendations

In all, the report makes 38 recommendations. More than half of them are relevant largely to the military environment, having to do with organizational and political approaches to change.

The remaining recommendations cluster around several important themes of interest to the broader data processing community. The themes of the recommendations are based on belief in the importance of:

- incremental development and prototyping
- reuse
- Ada
- 4GLs
- risk management
- metrics

For each of these topics, several recommendations are made.

Incremental development and prototyping. The report takes its strongest position in advocating a prototyping approach to incremental system development:

Recommendation 12: "Use evolutionary acquisition, including simulation and prototyping . . . to reduce risk."

Recommendation 23: ". . . mandate the iterative setting of specifications, the rapid prototyping of specified systems, and incremental development."
Recommendation 24: ". . . remove any . . . dependence upon the assumptions of the 'waterfall' model and . . . institutionalize rapid prototyping and incremental development."
Recommendation 26: ". . . provide . . . Product Development . . . with the ability to do rapid prototyping in conjunction with users."

Reuse.   The report is almost as strong in supporting the reuse of existing software components and systems:
Recommendation 29: ". . . develop economic incentives . . . to allow contractors to profit from offering modules for reuse, even though built with DOD funds."
Recommendation 15: ". . . direct Program Managers to assume that system software requirements can be met with off-the-shelf subsystems and components until it is proved that they are unique."
Recommendation 16: "All the methodological efforts . . . should look to see how commercially available software tools can be selected and standardized for DOD needs."
Recommendation 30: ". . . develop economic incentives . . . to encourage contractors to buy modules and use them rather than building new ones."
Recommendation 31: ". . . direct Program Managers to identify in their programs those subsystems, components, and perhaps even modules, that may be expected to be acquired rather than built; and to reward such acquisitions . . ."

Ada.   As might be expected, the report stands firm on the use of Ada as a standard military language. But it establishes some caveats for Ada's use:
Recommendation 8: "continue to forbid subsetting of the Ada language."
Recommendation 9: ". . . increase investment in Ada practices education and training, for both technical and management people."
Recommendation 32: ". . . establish a prototype module market, focused originally on Ada modules and tools for Ada . . ."
Recommendation 33: ". . . establish standards of description for Ada modules . . ."

4GLs.   The report is only lukewarm in its support of fourth-generation languages. Note the emphasis on "life cycle cost," a clear warning that both the productivity/maintenance advantages and the efficiency disadvantages of 4GLs must be carefully examined:
Recommendation 10: "Allow fourth-generation languages to be used where the full life-cycle cost-effectiveness of using the language measures more than tenfold over using a general-purpose language."

Risk management.   The report emphasizes the importance of new management approaches throughout. Here, however, it suggests a new management focus on risk in software development:
Recommendation 25: "... mandate risk management techniques in software acquisition ..."
An example of a risk management plan is included in the report:

1. Identify the project's top 10 risk items.
2. Present a plan for resolving each risk item.
3. Update the list of top risk items, the plan, and results monthly.
4. Highlight risk-item status in monthly project reviews.
5. Initiate appropriate corrective actions.

Metrics.   The need for a capability to measure software products and process, especially the quality of the product, is cited especially strongly:
Recommendation 18: "... devise increased profit incentives on software quality."
Recommendation 19: "... develop metrics and measuring techniques for software quality and completeness ..."
Recommendation 20: "... develop metrics to measure implementation progress."

Conclusion

When the smoke of all the recommendations is cleared away, the overriding message of the committee's report stands sharply focused: "We call for no new initiatives in the development of technology, some modest shift of focus in the technology efforts under way, but major re-examination and change of attitudes, policies, and practices concerning software acquisition."
In other words, technological breakthroughs are not going to be the salvation of software (nor, for that matter, is anything else). But changes in management approaches are needed.
Those may not be the words data processing people *want* to hear; but they are words we *need* to hear.
Members of the committee included such noted computing and software people as Vic Basili of the University of Maryland, Barry Boehm of TRW, Elaine Bond of Chase Manhattan, Neil Eastman of IBM, Don Evans of Tartan Laboratories, Anita Jones of Tartan Laboratories, Mary Shaw of Carnegie Mellon University, Charles Zraket of MITRE, and several government and contractor representatives.

From the Technical Trenches

The Cognitive View:
A Different Look at Software Design

The question I want to deal with here is "What is software design?"

That may strike you as an odd question to ask. After all, people have been designing software for 30+ years now. And don't we have all the design methodologies and design languages common sense says we need? So why, now, ask "What is software design?"

Well, the point I want to make is that all this time, when we've talked about design, we've been playing around on the periphery of the subject. Methodologies aren't design; they're frameworks for organizing our design efforts. Languages aren't design; they're representations for writing down the design once we get it. Design is something that happens inside the head, inside the brain, and it happens at a speed faster than lightning. It's *that* concept of design that I want to pursue here.

I've done my share of software design over the years, and I've taught the subject a few times, but I want to confess something to you. I've never felt that I really understood what design was, and whether what I was doing was the right approach to design.

In recent years, I've found I am not alone. While I was teaching software engineering in the graduate program at Seattle University, some of us avoided teaching design because we felt we didn't know what it really was, and therefore we didn't know how to teach it. Then I ran into some people during my year at the Software Engineering Institute at Carnegie Mellon who not only didn't feel they knew how to teach design, but in fact felt that no one knew how to teach it! At that point, I felt less alone, but I was still no closer to understanding what design really was.

Empirical Research Findings

All that is beginning to change. Other computing people who also felt that design is often an elusive subject have been conducting research into what it is. And they're beginning to come up with answers.

To understand what follows, you may have to loosen your grip on a few ideas that have become tradition in the short history of software. Quit thinking of external representations as what design is all about, and focus on mental process. Inside the mind lies the secret of design.

I still remember the occasion when that become clear to me. I was attending a class in the Ada language at the Air Force Academy. It was the last day of the week-long class, and the instructors had divided us into teams and given us a problem to solve. They had just finished laying out the requirements for us when one of my teammates, a bright young man from Boeing, came up with a design solution. Here I was, still trying to grasp the problem statement, and he had whipped through a design solution in his mind! It was then that I realized that design happened lightning fast inside the mind, and incidentally that some people's lightning struck much faster than others!

But what really happened inside that bright young man's mind? Answers to that question, at least the general question behind it, are beginning to emerge.

Before I talk about what those answers are, let me explain a little about where they're coming from. There's a new thrust emerging in software-related research, and it's from that thrust that the answers are finally coming. Researchers such as Bill Curtis at the Microelectronics and Computing Consortium (MCC) and Elliot Soloway of the University of Michigan (formerly of Yale) have long been interested in the idea that the study of software was at least as much about studying programmers as it was about studying programs. They've called this field of research "empirical studies of programmers," and the latest focus of this research area is on software design.

Confronted with the same question that I posed at the beginning of this article ("What is software design?"), these researchers laid out a plan for finding out. What they needed to do was to capture the thought processes of designers doing actual design work without intruding on, and therefore perturbing, the process. That's easier said than done.

But with the methods of a field called "protocal analysis" they have managed to do that. They have sat quietly with designers at work and prodded them to think aloud, recording what they say. They have audio taped design sessions. They have video taped group design processes. They have poured over the results of the recording process. And they have begun to formulate a theoretical description of what designers do.

The first set of things they learned wasn't all that illuminating. They found that design involved:

- understanding the problem
- decomposing the problem into goals and objects
- selecting and composing plans to solve the problem
- implementing the plans
- reflecting on the product and the process

All that was not very helpful. With a little tweaking of the words, in fact, that sequence is not much more than what we call the software life cycle, a thing we've known about and wrestled with for years.

It wasn't until they delved more deeply into "selecting and composing plans" from the preceding list that they finally struck pay dirt. Lurking inside that generic category was a simple set of steps that is the essence of design.

The Essence of Design

What were those steps?

The designers, mentally and at lightning speed, were doing the following things:

1. They constructed a mental model of a proposed solution to the problem.
2. They mentally executed the model—in essence, running a simulation on the model—to see if it solved the problem.
3. When they found that it didn't (usually because it was too simple), they played the inadequate model back against those parts of the problem to see where it failed, and enhanced the model in those areas.
4. They repeated steps 1–3 until they had a model that appeared to solve the problem.

Now, since those four steps are the key to the answer to our original question, let's spend a little more time on them before we move on. What we see here is a mental process, a very rapid process, an iterative process, a process in fact of fast trial and error. The mind forms a solution to the problem, knowing that it will be inadequate because the mind is not yet able to fully grasp all the facets of the problem. That problem solution, the mind knows, must be in the form of a model, because it is going to be necessary to try sample input against the model, run a quick simulation (inside the mind) on the model using the sample input, and get sample outputs (still inside the mind) from that simulation.

The essence of design, then, is rapid modeling and simulation. And a key factor in design is the ability to propose solutions and allow them to fail!

It is interesting to mention in passing that these same researchers have explored the problems of people who are not very good at design. Those people tend to build representations of a design rather than models; they are then unable to perform simulation runs; and the result is they invent and are stuck with inadequate design solutions. One of *my* favorite thoughts connected with these findings is that failure is an essential part of successful design! The end of every one of the previous iterations is a failed model, one shown to be inadequate to solve the problem; and that in turn suggests that an integral part of success is the ability to fail and to recover from it. I find that thought has intriguing implications from the point of view of teaching design, or any other subject for that matter. Where do we teach failure and how to recover from it?!

Several famous software designers have articulated some of these same ideas about design. In *Programmers at Work*, published by Microsoft Press from interviews conducted by Susan Lammers, they commented on the design process as they saw it, saying things like:

> "The first step in programming is imagining. Just making it crystal clear in my mind what is going to happen. In this initial stage, I use pencil and paper. I just doodle . . . because the real picture is in my mind." (Charles Simonyi, creator of Multiplan)

> "At some point, the [design] gets explosive and I have everything inside my brain at one time . . . . All sorts of things go on in my brain that I can't put on paper because I'm always changing them." (Gary Kildall, creator of CP/M)

> "You have to simulate in your mind how the program's going to work . . . . When you're creating something . . . and you have that model in your mind, it's a lonely thing." (Bill Gates, chief executive of Microsoft)

It is fascinating that the findings of the researchers in many ways match these informal quotations from well-known designers.

Some Other Findings

There is one other key finding about design that enters into this. Other researchers, such as Willemien Visser of Institut National de Recherche en Informatique et en Automatique, France, have found that "designers rarely start from scratch." That is, they use an existing model from a prior solution of a similar problem, as that first cut at the model that begins the simulation process. In fact, in retrospect, I think *that's* how the young man from Boeing ran such mental circles around me at the Ada class. He'd solved that class of problem before, and he had a tentative solution already lurking in his mind! (Isn't it amazing how well we can rationalize our personal inadequacies?!)

Now so far, this has all been about individuals doing design. But as we know, design in the 1980s has evolved into a team process. Problems have gotten too big for individual designers, and interdisciplinary problems cause a need for multiple and diverse skills among designers.

Those same researchers have been looking into team design. And they've found that, in many ways, it's a shared form of individual design:

- The teams create a shared mental model.
- Team members, sometimes in their own minds and sometimes in the group, run simulations against the shared model.
- The teams evaluate the simulations and prepare the next level of the model.

But in some ways these efforts are unlike individual design:

- Conflict is an inevitable part of the design process. It must be managed rather than avoided.
- Communication techniques become a vital part of the design process.
- Issues sometimes "fall through the crack" because no individual claims responsibility for them.

These teams of designers are typically 3 to 6 people. Sometimes, for enormously complex tasks, even that is not enough people. Then, design becomes an organizational problem. Typical organizational design evolves into a hierarchy of design teams, each with its own assigned problem subdomain, with an additional special team of chief architects whose job it is to hold the whole design effort together.

But design in team and organizational settings creates its own problems. Design can easily evolve into committee work, with all the disadvantages that implies (remember that the "camel is a race horse designed by a committee"). Fred Brooks, of *The Mythical Man-Month* and the more recent Silver Bullet paper, has pointed out that the best products we see, the ones that we agree have conceptual integrity (like Pascal and Unix), were designed by individuals. There *are* successful team designs, like Ada and COBOL and the IBM mainframe operating systems, but they are generally looked down on as being successful but clumsy, as Brooks points out.

Where Do We Go From Here?

So we have some new understandings. There is a well-defined process that goes on inside the mind during design. It begins with an existing or simplified new model, runs a simulation on that model, and continues iteratively until the design solution meshes with the problem to be solved. If the problem is big enough or complex enough, then teams or even organizations may do design. They use many of the same techniques as individuals but also use group process, a clumsy but sometimes necessary way to do business.

What do we do with these new understandings?

It seems to me that there are three categories to deal with that: the implications on the teaching of design, the implications on the doing of design, and the implications on the managing of design.

In teaching design, it is no longer enough to teach one or two or three methodologies and representations. Those older topics must be taught within a framework that includes the new concept of design as a mental process.

In doing design, it is helpful for the designer to understand that the heart of design is not what he or she thought it was supposed to be, and that the clumsy iterative process of trial and error that the designer is probably pursuing is actually the way it is supposed to be. That may give designers the confidence to pursue these appropriate design approaches without guilt. (Could we dare call this a "guilt-free" approach to design? No, that would be too much psychobabble!)

In managing design, managers can focus on communication facilitation and conflict resolution as their contribution to design. The empirical studies researchers further suggest that management of design should be the management of the key issues that arise during the design process.

In pursuit of these goals of better design education, practice, and management, several tool concepts are proposed by the researchers. We do not know how to build all of these tools yet, but if we did it would go a long way towards assisting the now-better-understood design process.

1. Modeling and simulation packages to support the mental process.
2. Idea archive and retrieve packages to prevent thoughts from falling through the cracks.

3. Strategic assumption surfacers that keep track of key requirements and pop them up when a candidate design is about to violate one.
4. Issue-based conflict resolution support.
5. Unresolved issue recording/tracking.
6. Mediated discussion support.
7. Group idea collection and coordination.

It may be premature, however, to talk about tools to support this process. We are just beginning to understand what design is really all about, after thinking we knew what it was about for over 30 years. Perhaps just that should be enough to absorb us for awhile. Figuring out what to do with that knowledge may be an issue for a later time.

We probably ought to have a handle to attach to this new understanding. The researchers call it "cognitive processes in design." I like that. It says the things that I believe should be said about design being a mental process.

This article, then, has been a look at the cognitive aspects of software design.

Some Thoughts on
Software Errors

This is a set of my personal thoughts, gleaned from over 35 years of experience in the industrial and academic worlds of software engineering. In these thoughts, I attempt to collect and focus some insight on the software engineering process and the software engineering product, using software errors as the magnifying glass through which the collecting and focusing occurs.

THOUGHT 1 *Not all software errors can be found by known error-removal techniques.*

This thought is about process. The known processes for removing software errors can be categorized as (1) review, (2) test, and (3) proof. We know a lot about the worth of these processes. All the levels of review, from requirements to code, have been shown to be the most cost-effective of the three. All the levels of testing, from unit to system, have been shown to be an absolutely essential supplement to review. Proof has yet to prove itself as an industrial-strength error-removal technique, but it offers a third and dramatically different alternative to the other two.

But what is really the important part of this thought is that no one of these processes is enough. Extrapolating that thought a little further, it is fair to conclude that . . .

There is not now a process answer to the problem of software errors.

THOUGHT 2 *Not all software errors are found EVER.*

This thought is about product. Many people believe that the software product is the most complex thing ever constructed by human beings. Certainly, when we look at the number of logic segments in a program, and then try to consider the labyrinthian paths made up of those segments, we encounter a combinatorial explosion and a near-infinity of different ways the executing program can proceed. Small wonder that error-free software has been an elusive target.

The thought that we cannot remove all errors from software is an important one. It does not excuse us from trying as hard as we can to remove all the errors—that is not the importance of this thought. What is important is that . . .

Software in critical systems must take precautions beyond error removal for defense against software errors.

That, in fact, is the reason we have the emerging and important discipline of fault tolerant software. Fault tolerance is the fallback solution when the inevitable error occurs.

It must be admitted that this is a controversial thought. Harlan Mills and others claim to be able to produce error-free software using properly psychologically-conditioned software engineers and disciplined use of certain processes. Perhaps they, unlike others who have made similar claims in the past, will be able to do what they say. But it is safe to say that both the state of the art and the state of the practice in 1988 demand that the possibility of latent errors in critical software must be dealt with.

THOUGHT 3 *Not all software error finders are equal.*

This thought is about the people who use the process to build the product. We have seen again and again that there are enormous differences between software developers, ranging in magnitude up to 30-1. Glenford Myers found that some software professionals discovered seven times as many software errors in a software product as others. Nancy Leveson found that only 9 of 24 participants in a software study found any errors at all in a software product with 60 known errors. The cover of Barry Boehm's *Software Engineering Economics* shows us very dramatically that the quality of software people has a far more profound impact on software productivity than any known software process.

What this thought tells us is this . . .

The most important element in software error removal is not the nature of the product or the nature of the process, but the choice of people.

Unfortunately, this thought does not tell us how to identify those people. We must still use subjective and ad hoc techniques to try to optimize our people choices.

THOUGHT 4 *Not all software errors are equal.*

This thought is about focusing the preceding thoughts. First of all, not all software errors are bad. Sometimes the benefit of removing an error is less than the cost of removing it. Furthermore, researchers such as Elliot Soloway who study what good software engineers do have found that good people tend to make more false starts than "bad" people. That is, at least early in the life cycle, the path to good software must inevitably lead through "errors" as ideas are tried and rejected. Here, we see clearly that some errors are not as bad as others.

More importantly, some software errors are much worse than others. Those are (1) the errors that persist through all the error-removal processes into the production use of the software, and then (2) cause the system of which the software is a part to do unsafe or expensive things. I showed in a 1981 study that these persistent errors tend to be where the software is less complex than the problem the software is to solve. For example, the software tests two conditions in an IF statement but neglects a third, or a logic branch fails to reset a variable it has used back to the value expected in the next segment encountered. Nancy Leveson has linked software errors and system safety, and has shown further that independent software developers tend to make common errors. Timm Gramms calls these "biased errors" and says that they come from "thinking traps."

The importance of this thought is that . . .

Both error removal and fault tolerance must concentrate on the worst of the errors—the ones that can result in unsafe systems.

Summarizing Thoughts

Through the magnifying glass of software errors, we can see and focus clearly on several important conclusions about software itself:

1. There is not now a process answer to the problem of software errors. It is not that we lack for process. We have
   • review, test, proof processes
   • requirements and structural testing
   • statistical and safety testing
   • unit, integration, and system tests
   • a plethora of tools and techniques
   The problem appears, simply, to be larger than any processes we know.

2. Software in critical systems must take precautions beyond error removal for defense against software errors. The product, for all of our efforts and all of our wishes, must be treated as if it still has errors in it.

3. The most important element in software error removal (and, for that matter, in all software work) is the choice of people to do the work.

Good people tend to find good solutions. "Bad" people tend to find MUCH worse ones.

4. Both error removal and fault tolerance must concentrate on the worst of the errors. Some errors appear to be easy to make; some errors appear to be hard to find; and some errors result in unsafe systems. More often than not, the easy to make and hard to find errors, in fact, lead to the unsafe system.

The news, then, is not as good as we wish it were. Software error removal and fault tolerance must employ

- carefully chosen people
- a variety of processes of known effectiveness
- understanding of the nature of errors and safety

Anything less than that is simply not good enough.

An Experimental View of
Software Error Removal

What's the most effective way of getting errors out of software?

What's the most *cost*-effective way of getting errors out of software?

Those are big-ticket questions. If you look at how the dollars are spent on software development, error removal is generally seen as *the* most expensive part of the software life cycle, beating systems analysis and design and coding each by a factor of something like 2 to 1.

Because those are big-ticket questions, I'm going to explore what we know about answers to those questions. What I'd like to be able to say is that we know Fact A, and Fact B, and Fact C, and because of that your best way to spend your software error removal money is to use Strategy Z. But it's not that simple.

Why isn't it that simple? Well, for one thing, there are a lot more opinions about the effectiveness of various things in software development than there are pieces of real and useful data. Perhaps even worse than the prevalence of opinions over facts, we have a lot of advocates in the software engineering business.

Because of all these opinions and all that advocacy, not only do we not have quantitative information on which to answer big-ticket questions like the preceding ones, but the whole atmosphere is emotionally charged. The advocates tend to grind a particular axe so thoroughly that either people flock to their side or are turned off by them. There is a large loss of objectivity when opinions and advocacy enter a picture.

But the solution to opinions and advocacy is objective data, right? Well, are there data to allow us to answer those big-ticket questions? The overriding answer to that question is *no*. It takes careful, controlled experiments to get facts and data, and hardly anyone is doing those experiments. Why isn't someone doing them? As we try to answer that question, things get even muddier.

One answer is that it costs a lot of money to do careful, controlled experiments. More money than the average researcher has. So much money, in fact, that hardly anyone is doing software experiments, especially where it counts most, in the world of large-scale software created by software practitioners. Not even those places where you might think these experiments *should* be done, like the government-funded Software Engineering Institute, or the industry-funded consortia like the Software Productivity Consortium and the Microelectronics and Computing Consortium (MCC).

But another answer is that there's a strange climate in the computer science and software engineering worlds, a climate in which the experimental component that is present in most other sciences and engineering is simply not present. The researchers who ought to be best qualified and most motivated to do software experimental research are simply not doing it.

There ARE Experimental Findings About Testing

Now all of that is a pretty depressing prelude to what I *really* want to say. Because in spite of all this gloom and doom about software experimentation, some of it has been done. And some fairly important experiments have been done in an attempt to answer questions about testing. We, in fact, have some experimentally-obtained answers to those questions. They aren't totally conclusive answers, but they're consistent enough that practitioners and their managers can probably start making decisions based on them. You *can*, in this case, use Facts A and B and C to choose Strategy Z.

And what makes this essay worth reading, if you're still with me at this point, is that the findings of those experiments are not only relatively consistent, they also point us in a different direction for software error removal than the one we currently tend to pursue.

What do we currently tend to do? Test the software hard, and then test it some more, and then test it again.

What do the experiments say we should do? Well, if our goal is to find the most errors and/or to get the lowest cost per error found, experimenters tell us that we should emphasize review processes more than testing. Design review, code review, test review—that sort of thing. As we will soon see, those approaches tend to unearth more errors faster and cheaper than does testing.

But wait! Don't go out and fire your independent test group and cut off the machine budget for your developers during checkout. The findings *don't* say to stop testing, period. They just say that testing isn't enough, and that reviews need to supplement testing. That's *still* a big deal finding, because in my experience not very many software developers do much design and code review work before throwing the new program in for testing.

So, enough preliminaries. Who are the researchers doing this experimental work, and what have they learned?

The Experimental Findings

I'm going to tell you about three different sets of people who have done experimental research in this area, all of them pretty much independent of each other except that the latest researchers have seen the published results of those who've gone before them. The people I'm going to talk about are:

- Glenford Myers of IBM Systems Research Institute, who published his findings in an article called "A Controlled Experiment in Program Testing and Code Walkthroughs/Inspections" in *Communications of the Association for Computing Machinery* in September 1978.
- Victor Basili of the University of Maryland and Richard Selby of the University of California at Irvine who did their work in conjunction with the NASA/Goddard Space Flight Center and published their findings in "Comparing the Effectiveness of Software Testing Strategies" in the *IEEE Transactions on Software Engineering* in December 1987.
- Jim Collofello of Arizona State University and Scott Woodfield of Brigham Young who did their work at an unnamed company and published their findings in "Evaluating the Effectiveness of Reliability Assurance Techniques" in the *Journal of Systems and Software* in March 1989.

There's the answer to the question of who the researchers are who do experimental work in this area. Now for the second question, "What have they learned?"

In order to answer *that* question, let's look first at what they *did*. Each set of people put slightly different English on their approach to the question.

Myers and Basili/Selby compared what some people call "functional testing" (testing to see if all the requirements are satisfied) with "structural testing" (testing to see if all parts of the program have been tested) and with code review. They performed their experiment on one or more relatively small programs using largely experienced practitioner subjects, having them look for errors known to be in the software.

Collofello/Woodfield broadened the base of the exploration and narrowed it at the same time; they used data from a massive real-time software project rather than conducting controlled experiments. And they did their analysis on design reviews versus code reviews versus something generically referred to as *testing*.

Each of the three sets of researchers was looking for the same kind of answers, but they each took a slightly different approach to measuring for those answers. All three, for example, wanted to get a handle on the *number* of errors removed and the *cost* of removing them, but Collofello/Woodfield designed new metrics for measuring counts and costs, which they called *error detection efficiency* and *error detection cost effectiveness*.

Now I know you're eager to get on with what these three sets of people found out specifically, but bear with me for one more detail. It turns out that, much as we wish it weren't so, the *way* you conduct research can have a major bearing on what you learn from the research.

To a certain extent, these findings compare some varieties of apples with some varieties of oranges. For one thing, whereas in a review process the reviewers tend to not only identify a problem, they also isolate where the solution to the problem lies; in testing (as conducted in these experiments) independent testers only identify that there is an error without isolating where the error can be fixed. Therefore, as experimentally measured here, the reviewers were doing more of the job than the testers were.

For another thing, in the Collofello/Woodfield research, which used project data, the testing took place after the review processes had removed a fairly large percentage of the errors, so that the testers were (1) looking for a different class of errors from the subjects in the other two experiments, and (2) possibly the errors remaining after the review processes were tougher errors to identify than those caught earlier.

Those kinds of differences may have an effect on research findings that ranges from trivial to profound. I only mention those here as an example of the difficulties involved in doing these kinds of experiments, and (more to the point) as reasons why using "facts" to choose "strategies" still should be done with caution.

And now (ta-ta!) specifically what did these researchers learn? First of all, regarding testing versus reviews, Basili/Selby found strong evidence that code reading was considerably better than both kinds of testing that they examined, and Collofello/Woodfield found that both kinds of reviews they examined were considerably better than testing. Oddly, the Collofello/Woodfield data were more conclusive in cost considerations than in count considerations and the Basili/Selby findings tended in the opposite direction. But nevertheless, these two sets of researchers came to the same overall conclusion—reviews beat testing.

Myers's findings are only partly in sync with the others on this matter. Myers found reviews and testing equally effective, and reviews more expensive than testing.

What about kinds of reviews, and kinds of testing? Well, there were more data gathered on kinds of testing. Basili/Selby found functional testing discovered more errors than structural testing, while Myers found them nearly equivalent. Regarding kinds of reviews, only Collofello/Woodfield looked at that, and they found design reviews much more cost effective in error removal than code reviews, but code reviews are somewhat more effective in errors removed than design reviews.

Now all of these words tend to muddy the picture of what we're learning here. Table 1 summarizes the findings of the three sets of researchers. In simplified form, here's what they seem to have learned, using a kind of majority rule argument:

1. Reviews are more effective than testing in error removal, and they tend to be more cost effective as well. The data here are not unanimous, however.

2. In kinds of testing, functional testing tends to find more errors than structural testing, and to find them more cheaply.

3. In kinds of reviews, design reviews are far more cost effective than code reviews, but code reviews tend to find more errors.

What does all that mean in terms of error-removing strategies? Probably something like this:

- Reviews MUST supplement testing.
- Testing must emphasize functions but not ignore structure.
- Reviews must cover both design and code.

Table 1: Research findings on error-removal strategies, review vs. test

Researcher ⟶ Measure ↓	Myers	Basili/Selby	Collofello/Woodfield
Efficiency	equal	1. code reading 2. function testing 3. structural testing	1. code review 2. design review 3. testing
Cost effectiveness	code review most expensive	code reading least expensive	1. design review 2. code review 3. testing (least)

Some Loose Ends

There are a few loose ends still to be tied up here. For example, what exactly did the researchers mean by functional testing and structural testing and code reading and reviews? It would be dangerous to go too far with strategies based on these findings unless we have a clear notion of what the findings are about.

Functional testing   uses the requirements specification of the program to define what needs to be tested. Myers gave the experimental subjects the specification and let the subjects decide how to use it for testing. Basili/Selby's subjects were asked to use equivalence partitioning (one test case representing a class of similar test cases) and boundary value analysis (emphasizing test cases at points where algorithms or methods change) as their way of developing test cases from the specification.

Structural testing   uses the internal working of the program to determine how to build test cases. Myers's subjects were given both the specification and the program listing from which to derive test cases in whatever way they wished. Basili/Selby's subjects were asked to make sure that each statement of the source program was tested by at least one test case.

Code review   is a static process (the software is not executed) in which participants examine the source listing looking for errors. The Basili/Selby subjects used a process they call *stepwise abstraction,* in which the prime subprograms of the software are identified, their function determined, and a composite picture of the whole software is determined from these individual functions so that these derived functions can be compared against the specifications. Myers's subjects, on the other hand, used *walkthrough/inspection* as their method of code review; it included individual code reading prior to the review, and some use of mentally walking test cases through the software's logic.

The Collofello/Woodfield paper did not specify the processes used in testing and reviews, but the description of the project in question (700,000 lines of real-time code developed in a modern high-level language by 400 developers, with quality assurance activities associated with each major phase of the life cycle) suggests that it either was a military project subject to the Department of Defense standards for reviews and testing, or one using similar standards.

Other Fascinating Miscellaneous Findings

For those of you who enjoy poking around in the dusty artifacts of experiments, there were other interesting findings, not previously summarized.

Basili/Selby found these tidbits of information:

1. The "number of faults observed, fault detection rate, and total effort in detection depended on the type of software tested." In other words, perhaps the choice of testing methods should be application dependent.
2. "Code reading detected more *interface* faults than did the other methods;" "functional testing detected more *control* faults than did the other methods." In other words, perhaps the choice of checkout methods should be dependent on the kinds of errors sought.
3. "When asked to estimate the percentage of faults detected, code readers gave the most accurate estimates while functional testers gave the least accurate answers." In other words, poking around in the code seems to give people a better perspective on what they've done.

Myers found these additional tidbits:

1. "There is a tremendous amount of variability in the individual results." In other words, *who* does the checkout may be more important than how it's done.
2. "The overall results are rather dismal." In other words, none of the error-removal processes, and in fact even combinations of the processes, was very good at identifying all the errors that were present.
3. There was "a negative correlation . . . between subjects' prior walk-through/inspection experience and their performance . . ." In other words, code reviewers may get tired of the experience over time.

Collofello/Woodfield also found additional information:

1. "Unfortunately, much of the data was inconsistent and unreliable . . . . The low number of data points seemed to mirror the disinterest of the developers in recording data . . . . No one checked the quality of the quality assurance data." In other words, even the use of project data is prone to problems in research analysis.
2. "The high [success] associated with the design review was surprising." In other words, a lot of errors were found very cheaply at design review time.
3. "Interestingly, one reliability assurance technique—testing—was not cost effective." In other words, testing, though necessary, is a pretty expensive way of doing business.

The bottom line of this essay can, in fact, be taken from the bottom line of the Collofello/Woodfield paper. "Testing must always be done, but organizations must recognize that the traditional emphasis of testing instead of reviews is not a cost effective approach."

In other words, the answer to those two questions we asked at the beginning of this article:

- What's the most effective way of getting errors out of software?
- What's the most *cost*-effective way of getting errors out of software?

is something of a surprise. It's not that we've been doing a bad job of answering them in the past; but there are some new answers that may cause us to revise the way we've been doing business.

And those answers are coming from the folks who, at last, are beginning to apply experimental techniques to the science of computer science and the engineering of software engineering.

The Many Flavors of Testing

There is evidence that testing is still vitally important to software development, and that it probably always will be. Reviews may be more cost effective, according to recent studies, and proof of correctness (if it ever scales up to larger problems) may be more rigorous, but neither can take the place of taking the software into a near-real environment and trying it out.

Once we realize that we are committed to a future full of testing, it is worth exploring what testing really means. I would assert that there are several flavors of testing, and that all too often when we speak of testing we consider far too few of those flavors.

Here are the flavors I see:

1. First of all, there is goal-driven testing. It is in goal-driven testing that the reason for testing drives the tests to be run. There are roughly four goals for testing:
   a. *Requirements-driven testing.* Here, enough test cases are constructed to demonstrate that all of the requirements for the product have been tested at least once. Typically, a requirements-test case matrix is constructed to ensure that there is at least one test for every

requirement. Tools are now available to support this process; 100 percent requirements-driven testing is essential for all software products.

b. *Structure-driven testing.* Here, test cases are constructed to exercise as much of the logical structure of the software as makes sense. Structure-driven testing must supplement (but never replace) requirements-driven testing because all-requirements testing is simply too coarse a level to insure that sufficient tests have been run. "Good" testing usually tests about 60–70 percent of the logic structure of a program; for critical software, closer to 95 percent should be tested. Testedness may be measured by a tool called a test coverage analyzer. Such tools are now available in the marketplace.

c. *Statistics-driven testing.* Here, enough tests are run to convince a customer or user that adequate testing has been done. The test cases are constructed from a typical usage profile, so that following testing, a statement of the form "the program can be expected to run successfully 96 percent of the time based on normal usage" can be made. Statistics-driven testing should supplement (not replace) requirements-driven and structure-driven testing when customers or users want assurance in terms they can understand that the software is ready for reliable use.

d. *Risk-driven testing.* Here, enough tests are run to give confidence that the software can pass all worst-case failure scenarios. An analysis of high-risk occurrences is made; the software is then examined to determine where it might contribute to those risks. Extra thorough testing of those portions is then conducted. Risk-driven testing is typically used only for critical software; once again, it should supplement, but not replace, requirements-driven and structure-driven tests.

2. In addition to goal-driven testing, there is phase-driven testing. Phase-driven testing changes in nature as software development proceeds. Typically software must be tested in small component form as well as total system form. In so-called bottom-up testing, we see the three kinds of phase testing discussed later. In top-down testing the software is gradually integrated into a growing whole, so that unit testing is bypassed in favor of continual and expanding integration testing.

a. Unit testing is the process of testing the smallest components in the total system before they are put together to form a software whole.

b. Integration testing is the process of testing the joined units to see if the software plays together as a whole.

c. System testing is the process of testing the integrated software in the context of the total system that it supports.

It is the manner of intersecting goal-driven testing and phase-driven testing that begins to tax the tester's knowledge and common sense.

For example, do we perform structure-driven testing during unit test, or integration test, or system test? What I would like to present here are thoughts on how to begin to merge these many flavors. Let us take a goal-driven approach first, and work that into the various phases.

Requirements-driven testing means different things in different phases. During unit testing, it means testing those requirements that pertain to the unit under test. During integration testing, it means testing all software requirements at the requirements specification level. During system testing, it means repeating the integration test but in a new setting.

Structure-driven testing also means different things in different phases. During unit testing, it means testing each of the lowest-level structural elements of the software, usually logic branches (for reasons that we do not go into here, testing all branches is more rigorous than testing all statements). During integration testing, it means testing all units. During system testing, it means testing all components of the system, with the integrated software simply being one or more components.

Statistics-driven testing is only meaningful at the integrated-product or the system-test level. The choice of which is application dependent; normally, the system level will be more meaningful to the customer or user.

Risk-driven testing may be conducted at any of the levels, depending on the degree of criticality of the system, but it is probably most meaningful at the system level.

There is one other consideration in testing: *Who* does the testing? Usually, all unit-level testing is done by the software developer; integration testing is done by a mix of developers and independent testers; and system testing is done by independent testers and perhaps system engineers. Notice, however, that whereas requirements-driven and statistics-driven testing require little knowledge of the internal workings of the software or system under test, structure-driven testing and risk-driven testing require software-intimate knowledge. Therefore, developer involvement in testing may need to be pervasive.

It is popular in some circles to declare testing to be nonrigorous, a concept on its way out. My view of testing is entirely the opposite. Properly done, testing can be rigorous and thorough. It is a matter of knowing how, and doing it. I hope this short discussion may set some testing concepts into proper perspective.

The Link Between
Software Quality and
Software Maintenance

What is software quality? Most commonly, it is defined as a set of attributes. If software is to be of good quality, then it must have:

- reliability
- efficiency
- human engineering
- understandability
- modifiability
- testability
- portability

What is software maintenance? It is the task of keeping software functioning to the satisfaction of a user.

It is interesting to note that, of those seven quality attributes, nearly all of them relate directly or indirectly to the key concepts in the definition of maintenance. Two of them, in fact, are specific to software maintenance and most of the others are critical to software maintenance. In other words, viewed properly, the task of building quality into software is almost the same as the task of making it maintainable.

That is an all too unusual view of software quality. Normally, we think of quality as an activity that developers create and quality assurance people monitor, almost for its intrinsic value. You build software? You give it quality, of course.

But that's a myopic view because the maintainability aspects of quality are the most difficult to achieve, and therefore the most easily forgotten when we see quality as kind of an "automatic" thing.

Let's look at the preceding key "ilities" to try to expand that myopic view to include maintenance concerns. The first two "ilities" that should catch the eye, from a maintenance point of view, are:

- *Understandability*—the ability of a reader of the software to understand its function.
- *Modifiability*—the ability of the software to be changed by that reader.

Now those two quality attributes are almost entirely about maintenance. Hardly anyone else needs to modify software, and few others need to understand it! (And certainly, they are also the quality attributes most difficult to assess.) What about the others? In order of interest from a maintenance point of view, they are:

- *Reliability*—the ability of the software to perform its intended function without failure. Now there's a key element in maintenance! If software isn't reliable, it's the maintainer's job to fix it.
- *Efficiency*—the ability of the software to operate with minimal use of time and space resources. Once again, that's as much about maintenance as it is about any development activity. Software that takes too long or grabs too much space will have to be shrunk by the software maintainer.
- *Testability*—the ability of the software to be tested easily. Usually we think of testing as a development activity, but certainly a large part of the maintainer's job is testing each change made to the product, and regression testing the things not changed.
- *Human engineering*—the ability of the software to be easily used. If the software is *not* easily used, who bears the brunt of the pain? The maintainer.
- *Portability*—the ease with which software can be made useful in another environment, such as a different computer or operating system. Once again, if software is ported, it may very well be the maintainer who gets called upon to do the job.

Not only are two of the quality attributes intimately linked to maintenance, but the others are linked solidly as well. Software quality, then, is as much about maintenance as it is about anything else.

In fact, there are other "ilities" of software quality that those involved with data processing usage talk about. They are the service attributes, related to the user's prime concerns rather than the developer's. They are timeliness, accuracy, reliability, and cost. Now the continuing achievement of those additional "ilities" lies entirely in the domain of the maintainer.

What's the point of these thoughts? Too often, software maintenance is an afterthought in everyone's definition of computing. Computer science and software engineering rarely talk about it. Until recently, tools and techniques were nonexistent, and even today research pays maintenance scant attention. Perhaps if we begin to see how important maintenance is to something right at the heart of the field of software, it will at last get the attention it deserves.

Barry Boehm has suggested that a key member of the software quality assurance team should be someone who will eventually maintain the product in question. Now there is a first step in the right direction. Not only does it work the problem, but it clearly relates the two topics of software quality and software maintenance that seem so seldom related to each other now.

Software Maintenance is a Solution, Not a Problem

Is software maintenance a problem?

Today's standard answer is "You bet it is."

The standard rationale for that standard answer is "Look how much of our budget we're putting into software maintenance. If we'd only built the software better in the first place, we wouldn't have to waste all that money on maintenance."

Well, I want to take the position that that standard answer is wrong. It's wrong, I want to say, because the standard rationale is wrong.

The fact of the matter is, software maintenance isn't a problem, it's a solution!

What we are missing in the traditional view of software as a problem is the special significance of two pieces of information:

1. The software product is "soft" (easily changed) compared to other, "harder," disciplines.
2. Software maintenance is far less devoted to fixing errors (17 percent) than to making improvements (60 percent).

In other words, software maintenance is a solution instead of a problem because in software maintenance we can do something that no one else can do as well, and because when we do it we are usually building new solutions, not just painting over old problems. If software maintenance is seen as a solution and not as a problem, does that give us some new insight into how to do maintenance better?

I take the position that it indeed does.

The traditional, problem-oriented view of maintenance says that our chief goal in maintenance should be to reduce costs. Well, once again, I think that's the wrong emphasis. If maintenance is a solution instead of a problem, we can quickly see that what we *really* want to do is more of it, not less of it. And the emphasis, when we do it, should be on maximizing effectiveness, and not on minimizing cost.

New vistas are open to us from this new line of thinking. Once we take our mindset off reducing costs and place it on maximizing effectiveness, what can we do with *this* new insight?

The best way to maximize effectiveness is to utilize the best possible people. There is a lot of data that supports that conclusion. Much of it is in the "individual differences" literature, where we can see, for example, that some people are significantly better than others at doing software things:

1. Debugging: some people are 28 times better than others.
2. Error detection: some people are 7 times better than others.
3. Productivity: some people are 5 times better than others.
4. Efficiency: some people are 11 times better than others.

The bottom line of these snapshot views of the individual differences literature is that there is enormous variance between people, and the best way to get the best job done is to get the best people to do it.

This leads us to two follow-on questions:

1. Does the maintenance problem warrant the use of the best people?
2. Do we currently use the best people for doing maintenance?

The first question is probably harder to answer than the second. My answer to that first question is "Yes, maintenance is one of the toughest tasks in the software business." Let me explain why I feel that way.

Several years ago I coauthored a book on software maintenance. In the reviewing process, an anonymous reviewer made this comment about maintenance, which I have remembered to this day:

Maintenance is:

• intellectually complex (it requires innovation while placing severe constraints on the innovator)

- technically difficult (the maintainer must be able to work with a concept and a design and its code all at the same time)
- unfair (the maintainer never gets all the things the maintainer needs. Take good maintenance documentation, for example)
- no-win (the maintainer only sees people who have problems)
- dirty work (the maintainer must work at the grubby level of detailed coding)
- living in the past (the code was probably written by someone else before they got good at it)
- conservative (the going motto for maintenance is "if it ain't broke, don't fix it")

My bottom line, and the bottom line of this reviewer, is that software maintenance is pretty complex, challenging stuff.

Now, back to the question of who currently does maintenance. In most computing installations, the people who do maintenance tend to be those who are new on the job or not very good at development. There's a reason for that. Most people would rather do original development than maintenance because maintenance is too constraining to the creative juices for most people to enjoy doing it. And so by default, the least capable and the least in demand are the ones who most often do maintenance.

If you have been following my line of reasoning here, it should be obvious by now that the status quo is all wrong. Maintenance is a significant intellectual challenge as well as a solution and not a problem. If we want to maximize our effectiveness at doing it, then we need to significantly change the way in which we assign people to it.

I have specific suggestions for what needs to be done. They are not pie-in-the-sky theoretical solutions. They are very achievable, if management decides that it wants to do them:

1. Make maintenance a magnet. Find ways to attract people to the maintenance task. Some companies do this by paying a premium to maintainers. Some do this by making maintenance a required stepping stone to upper management. Some do this by pointing out that the best way to a well-rounded grasp of the institution's software world is to understand the existing software inventory.
2. Link maintenance to quality assurance. (We saw this in the previous essay.)
3. Plan for improved maintenance technology. There are now many tools and techniques for doing software maintenance better. (This has changed dramatically in the last couple of years.) Training and tools selection and procurement should be high on the concerned maintenance manager's list of tasks.

4. Emphasize "responsible programming." The maintainer typically works alone. The best way to maximize the effectiveness of this kind of worker is to make them feel responsible for the quality of what they do. Note that this is the opposite of the now-popular belief in "egoless programming," where we try to divest the programmer's personal involvement in the final software product in favor of a team involvement. It is vital that the individual maintainer be invested in the quality of the software product if that product is to continue to be of high quality.

There they are . . . four simple steps to better software maintenance. But note that each of those steps involves changing a traditional software mindset. The transition is technically easy, but it may not be socially or politically quite so easy. Most people are heavily invested in their traditional way of looking at things.

If we are to get there at all, however, there is one vital first step which must be taken. It is the step that started off this essay.

We must see that software maintenance is a solution, not a problem. If we agree to that, then we have opened the door to profound changes in how we software people do our business. Think about it.

Single-Point Control

From a teaching point of view, science is made up of fundamental principles which can be separated out and taught as truth.

What are the fundamental principles of software engineering? Some people say that engineering is "soft science," that it is harder to identify fundamental principles.

I would like to nominate one such fundamental principle. My nomination for a fundamental principle of software engineering is what a colleague of mine, Lee MacLaren of Boeing Military Aircraft Co., refers to as "single-point control."

Single-point control is taking something which must be done several places, doing it in only one place, and referencing that one place whenever it is needed.

The most common example of single-point control is the program *module*, such as a library routine. If we need to take a square root or do a sort in several places in a program, we do not put the same identical code in all those places, but rather we put the code to solve the problem in one place and *invoke* it from the other places.

Why do we do that? Because it saves space, of course. Because it simplifies the logic, of course. Because if a change must be made in the code, it only need be changed in one place.

Modularization is just one example, albeit the most important one, of single-point control. What are some others?

Named constants allow the programmer to assign a name to a program constant and refer to it by that name throughout development and maintenance of the code. For example, suppose you are defining an array of size 100 in your program. In addition to the declaration of the array, you will probably loop on that array and add items to the array. From a programming point of view, this may look like

```
Array TABLE (100);

For I=1,100 Do...
TABLE[1] = something;
I=I+1;
If I > 100 Then Do-something;
```

Now, think like a maintainer, not a developer. Some day the customer may want that table to hold 150 things instead of 100. What will the maintainer have to do? Change the declaration constant 100. Change the loop constant 100. Change the table end test 100. Check for any other uses of 100 with this meaning, and change them. *Do not* change other, irrelevant uses of the constant 100.

What we have here is a situation where it is easy to make a mistake. That does not bode well for the quality of the revised software product.

Suppose, instead, we did this:

```
TABLE-SIZE Constant Integer = 100;

Array TABLE (TABLE-SIZE);

For I=1, TABLE-SIZE Do;
...
If I > TABLE-SIZE Then Do-something;
```

Now if the maintainer gets a request to change the table size, he or she need only change the declaration of constant TABLE-SIZE and recompile the program; if the developer has used the constant consistently, the other changes will be made automatically. Note that the opportunities for maintainer error are dramatically reduced.

Data declarations are another opportunity for single-point control. Take, for example, this code:

```
A = UNPACK(2,5,PACKED-DATA);
```

In many older programming languages, a function like that can be used to unpack bits 2 through 5 of the entity PACKED-DATA. If your programming language works like that, you may find it a fairly comfortable way to work with bit strings.

The problem arises if there is a lot of bit string work to be done in a program, and if the definition of those strings is likely to change over time. For example, suppose bits 2 through 5 of several different entities are referred to in a program, each with one or more UNPACK cells. And suppose then the nature of the problem changes so that the bit string becomes 2 through 7. Now the maintainer has the same kind of problem as before, but in a new context.

The best solution here is found in languages with a rich declarative component. In those languages, we may say something like

```
Record PACKED-DATA
FIELD Bits 2 through 5
End Record;
```

With appropriate additional language semantic glue, it is now possible to refer throughout the program to FIELD by name, and if the change of bit specification comes along we merely change the declaration, not each instance of a use of the declaration. The analogy to the benefits for *named constants* is apparent, even though the usage is somewhat different.

Table-driven code is code where the logic of a task is found in a declared table rather than in a string of procedural statements. Usually the table contains values, such as booleans or integers or character strings, which may be tested to direct the logic of the program.

With this approach, if the logic of the program changes, that change may be reflected in the data in the table rather than in procedural code (perhaps) scattered throughout the logic of the program. Again, what we have achieved is having one place in the program where a change will result in the automatic and consistent revision of many places.

A similar concept is *file-driven textual code*. With the advent of advanced and improved user interfaces (especially in micro software products), there is a new need for better control of user interface information. One approach to this problem is to enter *all* user interface text strings into a file, and have the program refer to this file when it needs such text.

The disadvantage of this approach is that it will take somewhat longer to fetch the text from a file. But the advantage is that the text is centralized in one place, and in fact is easily changed in that one place. For example, a change in the user interface of a program can be made by text editing the text file without touching (or recompiling) the program.

An interesting example of the use of this concept is the creation of a program which interfaces to users in different languages, such as English and Spanish. Now the creation of another foreign language version of the program is limited almost entirely to the creation of a new text file, not a program revision.

The efficiency disadvantage we mentioned previously is, in fact, easily overcome. Even though the user interface data are maintained on a text file, they can be read in at the beginning of execution by the program which uses them. The text may remain memory resident during execution, thus effectively eliminating the file overhead for fetching user messages as they are needed.

Single-point control is not just a programmer's concept, of course. In documentation we'd like to have one instance of a piece of information, and refer to it if we need it in one or more places. In data bases in particular, it is desirable to have a master set of data so that duplicate data sources do not begin to drift apart. In course development we'd like to make sure that the same subject is not taught in more than one course, and identifying a single point where the topic is taught is one way of heading off that problem.

There are a whole host of uses of single-point control. That's why it's *my* candidate for a fundamental software engineering principle. Now, what are yours?

User Friendly—Buzzword or Breakthrough?

User friendly is an expression we've all heard. It became one of the buzzwords of the 1980s, but is that all it is?

I vote "no" on that issue. Software engineers have begun to "think user." And the result of this thinking, I believe, is a true breakthrough in human interfaces for software. We have achieved here the most important progress in the computing field in the last ten years.

What do I mean, "think user"? The software engineer puts himself or herself in the place of the user, and develops the interface from that point of view. Some go so far as to say that the developer must start from the interface and work into the rest of the application, rather than the more traditional approach of starting with the technical problem and troweling the user interface on later.

User interfaces have become truly innovative, starting with the work at Xerox's Palo Alto Research Center ("Xerox PARC") and evolving on to the commercially successful Apple Macintosh. So called "windows" technology, where the user's display screen is treated as if it were the user's desktop and information can be overlaid over other information there, is now available for most computers from a number of competing software companies. Graphics interfaces have become much more realistic and the user can interact with pictures as well as words and charts. Animated graphics are not too far behind. Auditory output can be achieved with high quality if the customer is willing to pay for it, and although audio input is still fairly constrained, it has been successful where a constrained environment is acceptable.

It is important to note that there is a price for this exciting progress. The software engineer who wants a successful user interface must now expect to spend half again or perhaps even double the developmental time. User interfaces are becoming a specialty of their own; for products to be marketed to the general public, it may be necessary to bring in a human engineering specialist to design and perhaps even implement the interface.

How can a software engineer evolve the knack of "thinking user?" Paul Heckel suggests that the designer think like an artist, not a technologist, and treat the problem as one of communication. He suggests studying traditional art disciplines, such as movie making and entertaining, to find analogies to help the designer be more effective at thinking like a user.

"Think user" can take on many dimensions:

- market research—know your users and what they want and need (note that what they want and what they need may not be the same thing, but be careful about ignoring wants).
- user participation in reviews—let your users give feedback as the design evolves.
- prototyping—if the users don't have a clear picture of wants and needs, build them a sample and let them experiment with it.
- user education—help users get comfortable with the interface you eventually choose. Offer courses in product use.
- levels of user support—make the software self-instructional through a carefully constructed tutorial interface. Provide optional access to help files. Give the experienced user a faster interface option. Provide good user documentation to use when all else fails. Produce meaningful diagnostic messages.
- established guidelines for user interfaces—every publication on user interfaces (see the reference list) includes a set of 10 or a 100 guidelines for building good interfaces. Admonitions include simplicity, consistency, predictability, and so on. Find a set of guidelines appropriate to your application and follow it.

It is important for both the software engineer and the software manager to keep abreast of research literature and industry progress in this area. It is evolving so rapidly that the unaware specialist runs the risk of becoming obsolete.

If you want to read more on this topic, try these:

- ABLEX publishes a series of books on "Human/Computer Interaction," with such titles as:
  Advances in Human-Computer Interaction
  Human-Computer Interface Design Guidelines
  Directions in Human/Computer Interaction
- "Abstractions for User Interface Design," *IEEE Computer*, September 1985; Coutaz.
  Discusses approaches for successful *implementation* of friendly interfaces.
- *The Elements of Friendly Software Design*, Warner Books, 1984; Heckel. Says that good interface design is an art form, not a technology, and suggests that software engineers must study the techniques of such artists as movie makers. List guidelines for good interface design.
- "Design Guidelines for the User Interface to Computer-Based Information Systems," ESD-TR-83-122, 1983; MITRE Corp. The result of an Air Force funded study, this is one of the most comprehensive lists of guidelines available.
- "Designing the Star User Interface," *Byte*, April 1982; Smith, Irby, Kimball, Verplank, and Harslem. A list of the principles underlying the pioneering Xerox Star interface (which evolved to be the Apple Macintosh interface), written by the Xerox PARC system developers.

The Latest in Weaponry

Reuse: Software Parts— Nostalgia and Déjà Vu

The idea that software should be built up from off-the-shelf parts has received a great deal of attention in software literature (see [BELA80], [KERN76],[DENN81]).

It is an extremely attractive idea. First, the software builder can reduce both cost and schedule considerations since prewritten software is immediately available. Second, the software builder can simultaneously increase software quality, since pretested software is generally of higher reliability, at least, than freshly-written software. Since cost/schedule and quality are often competitors in a difficult and sometimes tragic tradeoff game, it is especially nice to find a methodology that enhances all of them. The notion of software parts, then, has a near-magic allure. In an era where "productivity" is the numero uno buzzword, software parts have to be a high-priority area of concern.

There are two ironies here. One, that the software parts approach is a bottom-up one and thus comes into conflict with the top-down approaches of the 1970s, is dealt with elsewhere [GLAS81]. But more ironic is that the software parts approach was at the very heart and soul of the software development industry over a quarter of a century ago. In fact, in the software parts area, our field has suffered a major regression over the years. It is vitally important to explore the issue of why.

Probably ninety-five percent of today's software developers were not in the field in the 1950s. Because of that, it is worth spending some time in an era long since past. What we will find, as the picture unfolds, is actually a prediction of the software parts era to come. We can, certainly in this case, learn from the past.

Stepping Into the Past

Come with me back to the computing shop of the 1950s. Ah, here's the door of the "Computing Laboratory." Let's step in.

Several things leap to our attention. Crewcuts on the programming men, bouffants on the programming women. The clatter of keypunch machines. The immensity of the computer room—all that square footage for a computer which, by today's standards, is truly tiny.

Those things may or may not be important from a nostalgic point of view, but from our technical point of view they are superficial. Let's look a little closer. There, on the desk of every programmer. What's that manual?

We pull it down from the bookshelf, noting that it says "SHARE" on the binding. Opening it, studying it, a light slowly dawns. This is a software parts catalog, and *every single programmer either has a copy or has access to one.*

"Where did *this* come from?" we ask a nearby young programmer. (Interesting—every one of them is young, you may have noticed. A brand-new field is like a positive magnetic field to youth . . . and like a negative one to experience!)

"Oh, that's the SHARE manual," he answers, offhandedly. "SHARE is our vendor's user group. We all contribute software routines to SHARE, and we all use what has been contributed."

"What about this page? It describes a uniform distribution random number generator. Where'd that come from?"

"Oh, that's from United Technologies. Fred Masner wrote it. In fact, he's written a lot of SHARE stuff."

"And what about this character string read routine?"

"Northwest Industries. Bill Clinger did it. His stuff is excellent, and it always works right."

Let's pause for a minute, digress from our sojourn into the 1950s. It's important to realize a couple of things. For one, there was no academic computer science world worth speaking about in the 1950s. That development was still nearly a decade away. Programmers emerged from mathematics training, or business administration, or even with English degrees! And that, in turn, meant that there was almost no computer science literature. A little bit of *Communications of the ACM*, but not much. A more universally-available *Datamation*. A doomed fledgling called *Software Age*. As a route to software prestige, publishing was a limited outlet.

There's a second point to be made here. Vendor software hadn't been unbundled yet. In fact, it hadn't even been bundled! Computer hardware often came with no software at all. And that's where the user groups, like SHARE, came in.

And in fact, that's why the name SHARE makes sense. It was a group for the sharing of software which was not really available from anywhere else.

Looking More Closely

But back to the 1950s. The SHARE manual, a collection of software parts descriptions, begins to make a little more sense. Now let's look at it more closely.

Up front, here, is the table of contents. Scanning quickly down, we can see a functional breakdown of software parts. Here's a section on Input/Output, another on Character String Manipulation, another on Mathematical Services, and many more. Let's flip back to the Math section, to see how an individual section is organized.

Again, we see a functional breakdown. There's a section on trigonometric routines, another on matrix manipulation, another on integration routines, still another on random number generation.

Well, let's look in even finer detail. What's at the bottom of this whole parts taxonomy?

This page looks typical. Hmm, here's a first paragraph describing the functions performed by the part. Then we have the author's name and corporate affiliation. Now there's a description of the input requirements and the output produced. And finally, a discussion of restrictions and miscellaneous notes. Usually, we see leafing through, there's one page per part. Sometimes, for the complex ones like I/O, there are two or three. Occasionally, when it matters, the underlying algorithm is discussed.

But always, near the top of the page, is the author's name and affiliation. And always, near the bottom of the page, is a disclaimer. "This software has been tested but it is not guaranteed to be free from error," or words to that effect.

"Is this stuff any good?" we ask the nearby programmer, wondering about that disclaimer.

"Yes, nearly always," he says. "In fact, if you read the code, you'll find it's usually—and I really hate to admit this—better than the best I can do. Most people don't contribute crumby stuff to SHARE because there's too much at stake. And we quickly spot the ones who do."

"Too much at stake." "Spot the ones who do." Another light is dawning. The building of software parts, in an era where there is little drive to "publish or perish," is the route to software renown and prestige in the 1950s. It's a highly individualized effort, the success route of the individual contributor. And there's an automatic screening out of the inept.

Let's browse the SHARE manual a little more. Sure enough, some names and affiliations recur about every fifth or tenth page. That's why our programmer friend immediately remembered the names of Fred Masner and Bill Clinger, and United Technologies and Northwest Industries. This is fascinating stuff. And a little mind boggling. Perhaps we should leave the 1950s for now, and digest what we have learned.

What Have We Learned?

Come back with me, back through the door marked "Computing Laboratory," back into the 1980s. What, in fact, *did* we learn?

First, there was a thriving software parts technology. Everybody expected to have prebuilt parts available to them.

Second, there was an effective parts taxonomy and an effective delivery document. If you wanted to find out what parts were available, it was easy to do.

Third, there was pride in software authorship. Parts appeared in the shared domain because there was strong motivation to do it. People got strokes from building software.

Fourth, there was no stifling counterinfluence. Software was not available "free" or at low cost from the vendor; it was either share or do it yourself.

Looked at in this light, the 1950s—that obsolete era out of computing's crewcut past—are a wonderful model for the present. What irony that where we are going is where we've already been. And now, it's time to return to the question, "What went wrong?"

I saw it happen. And it's a sad and frustrating story.

The most important thing that went wrong is an irony in itself. As the 1950s blurred into the 1960s, it was gradually becoming apparent that software was increasingly more difficult to produce. I/O packages might be SHAREd, for example, but could an operating system be? More and more, attendees at SHARE meetings (and at other user groups) pressed the vendors to deliver the software. And, eventually, they did. The SHARing of software atrophied . . . after all, couldn't Big Brother do it better and more reliably? SHARE meetings changed from a community of software users presenting and sharing solutions, to a clamoring hoard of users shouting "GIMMEE" to the vendors.

The SHARE manual fell into disuse, and finally vanished. In its place came a mile-long shelf of vendor literature. It emphasized the system, and often the use of tools within the system, but the notion of software parts except for a few things like math libraries simply disappeared. After all, a plethora of parts leaves a vendor open to a lot more user interaction and complaints. And can a vendor stamp that all-important disclaimer at the bottom of the writeup and legally get away with it?

A couple of other things happened, too, although their importance in the demise of the software parts community was less important. Computer science departments sprang up in universities across the land, and a theory of computer science gradually emerged. The energies that had gone into producing better software parts went now into producing better software theories. Belady and Leavenworth [BELA80] said it best:

> ". . . software engineering is polarized around two subcultures—the speculators and the doers. The former invent but do not go beyond publishing novelty, hence never learn about the idea's usefulness—or the lack of it. The latter, not funded for experimentation but for efficient product development, must use proven, however antiquated, methods. Communication between them is sparse . . .

I think we all hail the importance of the rise of software theory, but what we have lost and have not even mourned is acknowledgment of the importance of the doer of software as well. In fact, all too often the doer is the butt of negative published comments written by a speculator [DENN81].

The final thing that happened is the emergence of the "egoless programmer" concept [WEIN71]. Because ever-more complex software required ever more bodies to produce it, the notion of a team approach to software construction inevitably emerged. And in those teams, human ego seemed to get in the way of team progress. That was true, of course. What was missed in this concept, however, is that human ego is an essential drive which cannot be suppressed without bad side effects. Can you imaging, for example, an egoless manager? Or can you imagine an egoless theoretician, publishing articles in professional journals with no name and affiliation attached, and with no feedback to academic heads of department? We are all motivated powerfully by our egos, and if they are removed what results is a sense of lethargic irresponsibility.

Don't Worry Your Pretty Little Heads

And in fact, to complete the circle of this reasoning, isn't that precisely what went wrong with the old, true sharing SHARE? A strong authority (the vendor) eventually emerged and said "We'll take over all this software tools and parts stuff, don't you worry your pretty little user programmer heads about it." And with no ego-pull to contribute parts to a SHAREd library, the parts stopped coming.

So what can be done to hasten the software parts era of the 1990s? Learn from the 1950s, of course. At your computing shop:

1. Create a parts taxonomy and the shell of a parts document.
2. Invite programmers to contribute generalized parts to the shell.
3. Establish a reward system for parts contributors.
4. Distribute parts catalogs to all programmers.
5. Decide either to
   a. allow disclaimers on parts, with a low-cost "user beware" mode of operation; or
   b. establish a centralized parts certifying organization, with a high-cost but high-reliability mode of operation.

The result of this approach will gradually emerge. Within your computing shop—if not between computing shops—a thriving parts subculture will be developed. Out of that subculture will come a collection of parts provided by the people most likely to understand what parts are needed— the applications programmers. And out of the reward system will come a collection of top programmers, ego intact, who will have a new reason to feel proud of what they are doing, and visible rewards to show for it.

Déjà vu, 1950s. We know it can happen, because it all happened before. Just so.

REFERENCES

BELA80   L. A. Belady and B. Leavenworth, "Program Modifiability," IBM Research Report RC8147 (#35397), 3/6/80.
            Proposes an experiment in the value of data abstractions to enhance modifiability, using a 100k line operating system as the test bed.

DENN81   P. J. Denning, "Throwaway Programs," *Communications of the ACM,* February 1981.
            Recommends the creation of composable software parts to cure the problem of creating disposable software.

GLAS81   R. L. Glass, "No One Really Believes in Top-Down Design," *Software Soliloquies,* Computing Trends, 1981.
            Points out that design is often iterative, and that part of every design is bottom up.

KERN76   B. W. Kernighan and P. J. Plauger, *Software Tools,* Addison-Wesley, 1976.
            A description of a set of software tools, emphasizing their constituent parts.

WEIN71   G. M. Weinberg, *The Psychology of Computer Programming,* Van Nostrand Reinhold, 1971.
            Discusses egoless programming and individual ownership of programs.

Automatic Programming—
A Cocktail Party Myth?

It's not very often that something comes along in the serious computing literature that has a profound effect on what computing and data processing professionals do and think.

Perhaps the first of those I remember was in 1977 when Ben Shneiderman of the University of Maryland skewered the whole idea of flow charts via some experimental findings. In a very short period of time after the publication of his paper, the software world went from flow charting as a required design and documentation aid, to complete abandonment of the flow chart as being effectively worthless.

More recently, both David Parnas and Fred Brooks, in separate papers, threw gallons of cold water on the computer science research community, essentially saying that the breakthroughs in approaches to building software that many have hoped for are simply not going to come. The effect of those two papers is still being absorbed.

And now comes another. Two people from MIT, Charles Rich and Richard C. Waters, have tackled the area of automatic programming and reduced many of the claims for it to what they call "cocktail party myths," in a paper in the August 1988 *IEEE Computer.*

Cocktail party myths? What do they mean by that?

Well, for years, software researchers and software managers have longed for the day when programs would be written, not by programmers, but by other programs. This automation of programming would be the death knell for programmers as we know them according to the yearned-for goal. Some have even proclaimed that era to be already under way because of the use of fourth-generation languages.

And now, Rich and Waters, whose research into a "Programmer's Apprentice" has been at the forefront of this field, have thrown more cold water on many of their automatic programming colleagues.

According to Rich and Waters, there are several myths in the notion of automatic programming. They are:

- End-user-oriented automatic programming systems do not need domain knowledge. Wrong, they say. If there is to be an end-user automatic programming system, it must not only be an expert in program generation but in the application domain as well.
- End-user-oriented, general-purpose, fully automatic programming is possible. Not true, say Rich and Waters. All current automatic programming research leaves one of those three factors out.
- Requirements can be complete. Another myth. Requirements for problems of any complexity are incomplete approximations, subject to iteration to a final definition.
- Programming is a serial process. More myth! Programming is an iterative process featuring continual dialogue between end user and programmer.
- There will be no more programming. Yet another myth! End users will become programmers, marrying their application domain knowledge with newfound computing specialization.
- There will be no more programming in the large. The final myth. We will never settle for solutions to only those problems whose scope is so simple that they can be solved by a few people.

In other words, there are complexities in the process of writing programs that some researchers into automatic programming have tried to wish away. The contribution of Rich and Waters is simply to identify those things that cannot be wished away. After all of that, do Rich and Waters see any hope for automatic programming? Yes, but "automatic programming systems of the future will be more like vacuum cleaners than self-cleaning ovens," they say. Automation will help, but not replace, the person doing the programming.

The authors draw an interesting contrast between academic research, which has been ambitious but not terribly successful, and commercial products, which have set and achieved more modest goals. Systems are available commercially in these categories:

- Data base query systems which allow retrieval of information from a data base.
- Fourth-generation languages (4GLs) which allow quick-to-program solutions to narrowly focused problem areas at considerable inefficiency in the final program product.
- Program generators which are similar in concept to 4GLs except for how they are implemented (as translators to a compilable language rather than as interpreters).
- High-level design aids which are graphical tools to assist the designer in doing design.
- Project-management tools which support managers in task tracking.

Looking ahead, Rich and Waters still see "significant evolutionary progress" in pursuit of the automatic programming goal. But, like Parnas and Brooks before them, they see no breakthroughs here.

Some Thoughts on Prototyping

The software field spawns lots of areas of interesting controversy.

Prototyping is one of those areas.

It all began when some software academics and professionals questioned the idea of the "software life cycle," a series of steps through which, it was said, all software passed on the way from being an idea in someone's mind to being a functioning, computer resident solution to a problem.

The life cycle, some said, was a convenient way to describe what happens when software is developed. But unfortunately, some literalists seized on the concept and said that this was the way all software *should* be developed. The difference, though small in words, was profound in meaning.

Naturally, there was resistance to this bending of the life cycle idea. Dan McCracken, he of the 101 books on computing languages, and Michael Jackson, he of the data structure design concept, teamed to write a protest article, "Life Cycle Concept Considered Harmful." The controversy was finally out in the open.

Meanwhile, some practitioners and some theorists had been working with what appeared to be a diversion from the life cycle idea, the concept of "prototyping," that is, building a throwaway version of the software product in order to try out the development ideas before freezing them. Because prototyping appeared to be at odds with the life cycle concept, it became a part of the "life cycle considered harmful" controversy.

Controversy or not, software specialists continued to explore and expand the prototyping idea. One of the more interesting explorations was by Paul Heckel, who had been contracted to develop the software for a hand-held language translator, a word-at-a-time device which a world traveler could use to find out the French word for "hamburger" if an emergency arose.

No one had ever built a hand-held translator before, and Heckel's task was not just to build the software, but to build the software to support a marketable product. But what would make an unknown product marketable? A conveniently sized device with a readable display screen and user-friendly software which an occasional, novice user could employ without breaking out into a cold, electronic-aversion sweat every time it was to be used.

As it turned out, this was a tailor-made description of a project for which prototyping was the right approach. The problem Heckel faced, in a nutshell, was that the requirements were not well defined. What prototyping did for him was to allow him to experiment with a varying product which could be bent to explore varying requirements, leading to the point where the requirements could be frozen and a well-defined software product could be built.

Heckel, of course, was not the pioneer of the prototyping idea. But he was an early explorer, and his article, "Designing Translator Software" in the February 1980 *Datamation*, put the concept into a very real and visible framework.

Let's stand back a little, and look at what Heckel did, and the controversy of life cycle and prototype approaches. Recall that Heckel used prototyping to help firm up the requirements for a product. Or, thinking about what he did from a life-cycle point of view, he iterated in the requirements definition phase of the life cycle until he got them right, and then proceeded to go on to design and build the final product. Thus, the Heckel prototyping life cycle was requirements–design–implement–freeze requirements and discard product followed by requirements–design–implement.

Now if your point of view is that prototyping and the life cycle are in conflict, this is a clear example of how they differ. But it is possible to see what Heckel did as only a small variation on the traditional life cycle. Instead, the requirements phase was iterative, and involved some early design and implementation, before the remainder of the life cycle could proceed.

This view of a complementary relationship between the life cycle and the prototype approach is not a common one, however. The literature abounds with papers on the theme "prototyping versus specifying . . ."

In fact, in mid-1984 a pair of articles appeared in the literature experimentally exploring the differences between the life cycle approach and prototyping.

Now experiments evaluating two conflicting methodologies are few and far between in the software field, and these two papers should be applauded for their attempt to apply objectivity and dispassion to the controversy. The papers themselves were well written and interesting. It is just that while exploring the controversy, they tended to exacerbate it rather than diminish it.

What were these papers all about? Both of them documented an experiment conducted by the authors into what were the advantages and disadvantages of the two "competing" methodologies. The first, "Prototyping Vs. Specifying; A Multiproject Experiment," was published in the *IEEE Transactions on Software Engineering* in May 1984. The study was conducted by well-known software engineering specialist Barry Boehm and colleagues.

The second, "An Assessment of the Prototyping Approach to Information Systems Development," came out a month later in the *Communications of the ACM*, and was written by Alavi of UCLA.

The basic methodology of the two experiments was the same. Several teams of developers were used, some building a software product using the life cycle approach, and others using the prototyping approach. When the developments were all complete, they were scored on a well-defined set of criteria.

What did results show? To answer that question, user interviews and software developer interviews were conducted. The users generally found the prototype-constructed products easier to use, their reports more accurate and helpful, but (in the Boehm experiment) poorer in functionality.

The software developers found prototyping harder to manage and control, but with more coherent designs and programs which were easier to code and easier to integrate. Thus, in general, prototyping came out somewhat ahead, but with certain reservations.

So where does prototyping stand? In the middle of a controversy. There are interesting examples of its successful use; experiments which tend to reinforce that success, and some valid concepts.

How do you manage prototyping? How do you estimate how much to charge a customer for a prototype-built product, if you don't necessarily have a firm set of requirements? How do you avoid the "quick-and-dirty" first product becoming the final, poor-quality product?

These questions, controversy or no, remain valid. Even though it has been over ten years since Fred Brooks, in *The Mythical Man-Month*, told us to "build one to throw away," we're still not sure how to do it. We only know that it is a technology of promise, and the promise seems real.

Standards and Enforcers:
Do They *Really* Help Achieve
Software Quality?

Software standards are often seen as the most vital level of defense in the search for product quality. They are not. As used in practice today, they are more like a Maginot line, giving the illusion of protecting quality while actually hiding the fact that gross quality violations may be occurring.

What do we mean by software standards? These are the requirements placed on a programmer by organizational control structure, management, customers, or perhaps peers. They supplement the product requirements as stated in the requirements document, and have to do with the craft of programming, not so much the function of the final product.

It is important, when talking about standards, to talk also about enforcers. By enforcers we mean methods which check for standards conformance. It is important to discuss the two together because standards which are levied but not enforced result in the same thing as no standards at all.

The purpose for having standards is to increase product quality and programmer productivity. Standards, for example, may specify ways of naming data variables. Such a naming convention increases productivity and improves quality because it lessens the chance of committing time-wasting errors in naming variables, and increases the readability of the resulting program to the benefit of the checkout specialists and the maintainers.

Typical standards might include:

- language requirements
- limits on code complexity
  - structured programming constraints
  - avoidance of undesirable language forms
- requirement for modality
- requirements for maintainability
- naming conventions
  - data names must reflect the content of the variable OR
  - data names must reflect the structure of the program and data OR
  - some combination of both of the preceding
- commentary conventions
- code elements traceable to design or requirements
- interface structures

It is the task of a standards enforcer, then, to check for conformance to as many of the standards defined in the standards manual as is possible. That is easier said than done. Enforcers may easily check for limits on code complexity, for example, but checking for the use of meaningful variable names has semantic implications and can only be done by a human being. Typically, automated standards enforcers can detect less than half of standards violations, and the use of a human enforcer is essential.

Where do standards come from? While there are international bodies to propose standards of general usefulness, the present state of the practice is that most standards are home-grown.

What's Wrong With this Picture?

There are two serious problems with the use of standards and enforcers in current practice. The first is the most computing installations have too many standards. The second is that most computing installations do almost no enforcing. The two problems are related.

In most programming shops, if there is a standards manual at all it is probably at least 100 pages long, chock full of wonderful rules for building software. It was probably written by a group of people who either (1) could be spared from writing software because their talents were not in as high demand as their peers, or (2) had developed what they perceived to be a "best" way of writing software and wanted to make sure that everyone else did it their way.

All of this is the wrong way to establish software standards.

First of all, standards should be terse and to the point. The *must* rules for writing software, no matter what the installation, should be distilled into a short manual which can be digested quickly, applied easily, and enforced conveniently. If there are more elaborate, preferred but not required ways of building software, a different document which specifies *guidelines*, not *standards*, should be established. This document may be as long as it needs to be, because it contains helpful hints which most programmers will want to read, and length will be less of a problem since there is no need or even intention of enforcing these rules.

Second, standards should be written and reviewed by the best programming talent in the shop, not by whomever happens to be available at the moment. Rules on which a great deal of emphasis and enforcement is to be placed deserve the best knowledge available.

Third, enforcement of standards should be mandatory, not something done if there happens to be time. Once the decision is made to shorten the standards document to only what is really essential, the pain of enforcement diminishes rapidly. Enforcement processes should include automated enforcers where possible (these are sometimes called *code auditors*), and the use of reviews as necessary where automation is not possible. Peer code reviews are one important way of doing standards enforcement, although the main focus of such a review should be on quality as a whole, not just standards enforcement.

There is another problem in the area of enforcement. Often quality assurance organizations will perform standards enforcement activities, and pronounce the software to be of high quality.

It is important to distinguish between standards conformance and product quality. Standards are a narrow subset of the total issue of quality, and although it would be nice to establish the definition of quality in terms of conformance with a sufficient set of standards, it is simply not possible. Software quality is defined in terms of attributes such as portability, efficiency, human engineering, understandability, testability, modifiability, and reliability. And if you think about ways of demanding achievement of those attributes in terms of rules, you will quickly see the software quality cannot simply be legislated, it must be performed. Efforts to measure quality in terms of standards conformance are doomed to letting poor-quality software slip through undetected.

So what is the bottom line on standards and enforcers? They do indeed help software quality and software productivity. But they must be done right. There are many pitfalls along the way, and many people *aren't* doing them right.

Are you?

Recommended: A Minimum Standard Software Toolset

The tools world has exploded in the last few years. CASE tools in astounding numbers are now in the marketplace. The "Guide to Software Productivity Aids," a tools catalog from Applied Computing Research, is over 300 pages long and lists 25 *categories* of tools.

And yet there is something missing in all of this plethora of tools. It's the same thing that was missing a decade ago when I first wrote an article with the same title as this one (it was published in ACM SIGSOFT's "Software Engineering Notes" in October 1982).

What's been missing and is still missing is the notion of the minimum toolset that all software developers ought to have to build software, no matter what methodology or application domain they are involved with.

It's the hammer, screwdriver, and pliers look at software that I advocate here. At the top of the programmer's toolkit, in the place where the most frequently used tools are found, should be the same set of capabilities that all other programmers have in *their* toolkits. And the big question of the tools day, as far as I'm concerned, is not "How can I get lots and lots more tools?" but "What are the essential tools that I ought to buy?"

The former question leads to the current tools situation—great sales for tools vendors, but a lot of "shelfware." (Shelfware is a collection of tools bought and put on the shelf to gather dust because it simply didn't prove useful in the user's own world).

What I advocate here, and what I have been advocating for longer than I wish it were necessary, is the definition of this essential (read "standard") set of tools.

Standardization? Isn't that a frightening word? Well, yes, in some ways it is. In my worst standardization nightmares I envision a lockstep group of marchers, moving indistinguishably toward an uninteresting goal. But in my most positive view, I also acknowledge that standardization can be a dependable light at the end of a murky tunnel.

Consider the light bulb as an example of standardization at its best. The shape and size of the base is standardized; the shape and size of the globe is not. Standardization of the base was essential to the creation of a *profitable* light bulb industry. Omitting standardization of the globe was essential to the creation of a *creative* light bulb industry. Standardization, properly done, can stimulate both profit and creativity. That analogy should be useful to us as we begin to think about what to standardize in the software tools business. Clearly, "lean" standardization is preferable to "fat" standardization.

Let me illustrate the value of a universally-available, minimum standard toolset with an anecdote. Some time back, I took over responsibility for an existing software program. The program was disabled; that is, another programmer had revised the program and somehow disabled it in the process. My task was to get it working again.

There is a tool which can quickly attack just this kind of problem. The comparator, which compares two files to identify the differences between them, can be used to spot changes from one version of a source program to the next. The programmer who had done the faulty revision was apparently not aware of the existence of such a tool. Employing an available comparator, I was quickly able to see that in addition to the more meaningful changes the previous programmer had made, he had inadvertently deleted the key word ELSE from the middle of an IF statement. A problem which had seemed serious and consumed a great deal of the previous programmer's time was quickly solved.

The point of the story, of course, is that if all programmers were aware of the existence of certain fundamental tool capabilities, including the comparator, then some things that are now hard would become much easier. I would assert that the comparator is a leading candidate for a minimum standard toolset.

"But don't we already have that?" you might ask. "When we read the literature or talk to a CASE vendor, aren't we all talking about basically the same set of functional capabilities?"

The answer is a resounding "No." My first exposure to this "No" resulted from a literature search I conducted when I wrote the previously mentioned earlier paper. I looked at 16 toolsets in the literature, and 38 functional capabilities. Then when I drew a matrix of toolsets versus functions I found not a common base of functions across all toolsets, but rather a wide scattering of them.

If you were to perform the same analysis against tools available from CASE vendors today, you'd find the same situation. The good news is there are lots of tools available now that were not available a decade ago. The bad news is that there is no minimum standard set of functions available from anyone.

To be sure, most companies buying tools have decided on the set of capabilities *they* would like to have. But each company tends to make a different set of choices.

One bright spot is happening at the U.S. Government Services Administration, which has chosen a set of tools called "The Programmer's Workbench" for use at all government agencies. But even here, although the set of tools is carefully chosen and integrated, there are overlapping functional capabilities among tools in the set. Some functions that others might see as fundamental have been left out.

The GSA Workbench includes these tools:

- Rand Development Center, to integrate the other tools
- ANALYZER, a test coverage monitor
- TRANSIT, a COBOL-COBOL translation system
- DCD II, a cross reference list capability
- RETROFIT, a COBOL restructurer
- CSA, a data name standardizer
- HAWKEYE, a COBOL reformatter
- DATA-XPERT, a file/database manipulator
- PATHVU, a metrics analyzer
- COMPAREX, a file comparator
- VIA/INSIGHT, a source code analyzer

To learn more about the Programmer's Workbench, contact
Government Services Administration
Office of Software Development and Information Technology
5203 Leesburg Pike, Suite 1100
Falls Church, VA 22041

If the greatest need in tools is not frills but fundamentals, how can we move to identify those fundamentals? Unfortunately, different writers will still tend to take different views of this question.

In what follows, I would like to propose, in life cycle phase order, the set of tools that I believe everyone ought to be buying for their software developers, no matter what operating system or computer hardware is being used. With that generality in mind, I can, of course, only mention functional capabilities, not specific tools. The existence of a specific tool to match each functional capability is up to the marketplace for the particular environment in which your organization functions. But my hope in defining such a list is to

- allow you to decide whether this set of tools matches the needs of *your* organization
- give you the beginnings of a shopping list as you go to see what is available
- encourage tools vendors to fill in the missing gaps of these functional capabilities for product lines on which they are not presently available

In any case, here is my proposal for a minimum standard software toolset:

Requirements Definition

Requirements representation processor   a tool that automates the representation of requirements. The most common such representational techniques these days are data flow diagrams and structure charts. But here is a case where the selection of a particular tool must match methodological choices presumably already made at your company.

Data dictionary/repository   a tool that provides a central place for defining and referencing system data.

Design

Design representation processor   a tool which performs the preceding requirements function for design. One common design representation, the textual Program Design Language, can be supported by tools that not only construct the design representation but check it for consistency and perform cross-references on it. Again, the choice of tool is dependent on a methodological choice presumably already made.

Implementation

Conditional compilation   a tool that enables marking certain source statements for inclusion/exclusion at source compilation time based on conditional selection criteria. For example, a single source file might contain multiple versions of a program—a production and a debug version, or a PC and a MacIntosh version. Conditional compilation tools allow the selection of the version desired as the program is being compiled.

Checkout

Source debug   a tool that allows debugging of a program in the same language in which it was coded (variables printed with their names and formatted values; traces of variables of concern; breakpoints; and so on).

Interactive debug   a tool that provides the preceding services and in addition allows the debugging person to interact with the executing program.

Maintenance

Global cross-reference list   a tool that allows locating all references to any named entity, such as a data variable or a routine, anywhere in the source code of a software system.

Call structure generator   a tool that shows what routines call and are called by other routines.

Timing/performance analyzer   a tool that allows locating resource consuming portions of programs.

Management

Configuration management   a tool that allows baselining and reconstructing of software and documentation from protected versions.

Documentation

Word processor   a tool that allows creation and maintenance of computer-based documentation.

Multipurpose/miscellaneous

Data base/file manager   a tool that allows easy construction of and access to masses of fundamental and interrelated data.

Text editor   a tool that allows creation and maintenance of computer-based text.

File compare   a multifunction tool that provides for

- identifying differences between source text versions (either source code or documentation).
- identifying differences between current test case results and previous, baselined and correct test case results.

In the preceding material, I have defined what I believe to be the minimum essential set of tools that any software shop should make available to its software people. It is my intent that this list be a starting place and not an ending place, and that more tools than this minimal set be bought (keeping in mind the unique needs of your organization, methodology, computing system, and environment).

I even hope that other writers will take issue with my set of choices, and add important capabilities of their own to my list (keeping in mind that a minimum standard list should be as lean as possible).

I still believe very strongly that it is here, at the *minimal* end of the toolset business, that we need definitive work, before the wonderful work happening at the *maximal* end of the toolset business diverts us from what our needs really are.

Just in CASE:
A Look at
Software's Latest "Breakthrough"

Breakthrough! Salvation! Miracle!

The claims make it sound like the software panacea has been found again.

What's the panacea this time? It's CASE (Computer Aided Software Engineering), and it's supposed to shrink the data processing applications backlog almost as effectively as applying a pin to a balloon.

Won't we ever learn? Why do we keep looking for universal elixirs? Why do we continue to neglect the words of experts like David Parnas (there are no software breakthroughs coming soon) and Fred Brooks (there are no "silver bullets" for slaying the software "werewolves")?

The fact is that software development is the hardest intellectual challenge humanity has ever undertaken, and to expect panaceas is to wish away that fact.

The fact is that productivity progress is going to have to come from people and not tools and methodologies. (The cover of Barry Boehm's book *Software Engineering Economics* shows us that very graphically.) And continuing euphoria over tools and methodologies diverts us from potentially more profitable directions.

The fact is that we're looking for a complete shopsmith toolset when we haven't even settled on a definition of the minimum software toolset, the hammer, pliers, and screwdriver of software.

And the fact is that we have no metric data defining how software is built now, so we have no way of measuring a breakthrough even if one met us in the roadway!

In short, we're being hyped again, by the hucksters who put every STRUCTURED poobah and ARTIFICIAL intelliwax into some unreachable pedestal where reality always smashes expectations. I'm mad, and I don't want to take it any more!

Who are these purveyors of panaceas? They're a strangely mixed crowd, a noncoalition of two groups who hardly know they're in the same bed together:

1. *The entrepreneurs.* These people are good at what they do. They sell knowledge to the sophisticate and snake-oil to the naive. They take goodness and turn it into greatness whether it deserves it or not. Generally, they're wise enough to know goodness from greatness, but they're also wise enough to know that goodness doesn't sell.

2. *The computer science researchers.* These people are also good at what they do. They conceive of new ideas and then assume, without experimental evidence, that their new idea is greatness. Generally, they genuinely believe that their goodness is greatness. In addition, they are wise enough to know that goodness doesn't attract research grants.

Want an example of how it all works? The computer science researchers tell us that automatic generation of code from requirements specifications is right around the corner. To show that they're right, they build prototype tools to demonstrate that they've done it. If you look closely, you'll find that their requirements specifications look a lot like design, bordering even on code. Given *that* trend, automated generation of code from code-like specifications *is* right around the corner! But it doesn't mean much.

Then the entrepreneurs come along, point to the researcher findings, and claim that they're offering automated code generation from specifications *now*. They even imbed the capability in a CASE. The right claim. The right reasons. The right product. Who would be oafish enough to say "Nay" to brilliant research and brilliant marketing?

The un-hyped case for CASE

It's a darned shame. There's substance in the small to all these largesse in the large claims. Structured programming and artificial intelligence and—yes—CASE are worth something. Trouble is, we don't know how much. The best guess we have, from experiencing the technology and reading the literature and tracking the experiments, is that each of these "breakthroughs" can add an improvement of 2 percent to 20 percent to our ability to build quality software productively. (How can you move toward the 20 percent? By having particularly poor software developers to begin with! Not what you wanted to hear, was it?)

Given that there is value to CASE, let's look a little more closely at what CASE is. If you look at the collection of current products that claim to be CASE, there's not much consistency to what's there—yet. But if you step back a little from those products to see where they claim to be going, we do find some commonality.

CASE, someday, will be

- Systems analysis assistance in the form of automated requirements organizers (e.g., a tool that draws and consistency/accuracy checks data flow diagrams).
- Requirements/design experimentation assistance (e.g., a tool that assists the generation of prototypes of user interfaces or models of rudimentary requirements solutions).
- Design support assistance (e.g., a data dictionary package or a program design language checker).
- Coding support assistance (e.g., a code generator back end for a problem-oriented front end).
- A common human and internals interface which ties these tools together, and makes it convenient to use them as a toolset.

In short, CASE will be an integrated, full life cycle toolset to support the software construction process. Pretty neat, huh?

And maybe, taking those five preceding bullets and being generous and giving each one a 5 percent benefit, we can get a 25 percent quality/productivity improvement out of a carefully constructed and chosen CASE. Again, pretty neat.

But not a breakthrough. Not a salvation. And *certainly* not a miracle.

Looking at the Numbers
CASE and 4GLs:
What's the Payoff?

How much benefit can we expect from automated software development approaches?

That's an important question. We are spending a lot of money and energy moving the software field towards automation, through methodologies and CASE tools and 4GLs. Is the payoff commensurate with the cost?

Unfortunately, there are far too few attempts to answer that question. Getting an answer involves somehow examining new technology versus old technology costs, and no matter how you go about it, it gets to be expensive.

Nevertheless, what I present here are three studies that shed some light on this issue. One study involved a survey, another involved an experiment, and the third involved a case study.

And when we've finished looking at those, we'll take one last over-view look based on some opinions and survey findings.

These studies involve the value of 4GLs and CASE tools. And before I give you the results, let me say that studies of this type are still inexact in our immature field. A lot more work of this kind needs to be done to get answers we can depend on.

But with that warning, let me give you the bottom line:

1. One particular CASE tool gave improvements of 9 percent in cost and a similar improvement in quality over traditional approaches.
2. A pair of 4GLs produced code 29 to 39 percent shorter than COBOL, but roughly 50 times slower.
3. Another 4GL reduced development effort by 4 to 5 times the comparable COBOL estimated effort.

Before we go into detail about how these numbers were obtained and how to interpret them, let's step back a little and look at the results.

First of all, this is hardly the stuff of which breakthroughs are made. Improvements of anything in the 10 percent to 100 percent range are nice to have, and worth paying something to get, but are certainly not the "order of magnitude improvements" that some hucksters and researchers have been claiming. Even the 4 to 5 times improvement, which is considerably at odds with the 29 percent to 39 percent improvement (given that both relate to how much faster one might write 4GL code than COBOL code), is still not an order of magnitude better than its alternative. The message to date is clear: Automated software development approaches are worthwhile but not essential.

Now, let's look a little more deeply into the studies themselves. There's more information to be gleaned than the brief overview just presented.

CASE Tool Results

The CASE tool study is documented in a paper (which had not yet been published at the time of this writing) called "A Survey on Applications of a CASE Environment: Insights Gained," by Rudolf Lauber of the University of Stuttgart and Peter Lempp of SPS Software Products and Services. It explores the use of a European CASE tool called EPOS in largely real-time applications in West Germany.

EPOS, at the time of the study, was a CASE tool with features to support much of the front end, middle end, and management of the software life cycle, but it lacked a couple of important features that have since been added such as graphical representation and automatic code generation. Nevertheless, it offered facilities for requirements organization and specification, conceptual design definition and refinement, feasibility analysis, preliminary and detailed design representation, and documentation and quality support.

The study of the value of EPOS was conducted by survey and interview. Twenty-two managers of medium-large scale projects at 14 companies were involved. Most of the projects had not yet moved from development into maintenance. The survey was comprehensive, and the interviews were lengthy (typically, a half day).

What were the findings?

1. The greatest benefits were perceived to be in project management and control.
2. Costs tended to increase at the front end of the life cycle, decrease at the back end (with a projected huge improvement in maintenance and documentation costs), with an overall net saving of 9 percent.
3. Fewer errors during the front-end processes were reported by 69 percent of the projects.
4. Most documents (75 percent) were produced automatically by the tools.
5. Creativity and motivation of technical people were not influenced at all.
6. Acceptance of the tools ranged from enthusiastic at the outset, to disillusionment during training, back to enthusiastic after some usage.

Overall, how did the authors summarize their findings? "The net savings estimated was far from dramatic: Certainly no one observed costs to diminish by an order of magnitude." The tools produced "evolutionary rather than revolutionary cost reductions."

3GL versus 4GL Experiment

Second, let's look at the 3GL versus 4GL experiment. Santosh Misra and Paul Jalics of Cleveland State University published their findings, "Third-Generation vs. Fourth-Generation Software Development," in the July 1988 *IEEE Software*. They wrote a small-medium business application three ways: once in dBase III, which they called a "low-level 4GL;" once in PC Focus, which they called a "higher-level 4GL;" and once in COBOL. dBase is, of course, a data base tool with both procedural and nonprocedural capabilities for report generation; PC Focus is a nonprocedural language that runs on microcomputers.

The results were disappointing from the 4GL point of view:

1. 4GL source codes were only 29 percent to 39 percent smaller in length than COBOL.
2. The source code advantage for 4GLs would be improved if data declarations were also considered (the 4GLs required few if any), but most software engineers today believe that having data declarations is better than not having them.

3. Development time was 15 percent faster for dBase III than COBOL, but 90 percent slower for PC Focus (even when most learning curve costs are substracted out).

4. Performance of the 4GL codes were 15 to 174 *times* slower for the 4GLs than for COBOL.

The authors concluded ". . . development time . . . savings were not substantial," "performance . . . was clearly much worse than . . . COBOL," and ". . . if you cannot solve your problem readily with non-procedural features . . . you must write programs in some very strange languages—some of which are actually a step backward from 3GLs." In other words, the dramatic benefits of 4GLs, if they are achievable at all, only occur when the 4GL closely matches the application. Not a very encouraging picture.

3GL versus 4GL Case Study

The final set of findings were published in the same journal (*IEEE Software*, July 1988). June Verner and Graham Tate of Massey University in New Zealand looked at "Estimating Size and Effort in Fourth-Generation Development." The main focus of their study was on the usefulness of present-day estimation techniques for 4GL developed applications. (Basically, they found them wanting.) But along the way, in the context of a small business application, they found considerably more advantage to their 4GL than the previous authors.

Here, the 4GL was ALL, Microdata's Application Language Liberator, chosen after a competitive process with their specific application in mind.

Their relevant findings were fairly crisp: Effort for the 4GL implementation versus the estimates for a comparable COBOL implementation favored the 4GL approach by 400 percent. If feasibility and requirements were factored out (because the time to do them should not be dependent on the language chosen), the savings were 530%.

These findings are the more impressive because the authors expressed skepticism about vendor claims for productivity improvements at the beginning of their case study. Although they found, like the previous authors, that complex things were very hard to do in the 4GL, the bottom line was a significant (though not order of magnitude) improvement.

So there are some research findings on the use of specific software automation tools. They're not terribly showy, but then they're not shabby either. Is there any perspective we can get elsewhere?

In "Who's Winning the CASE-4GL Race?" (*System Builder*, March 1989), John Kador reports that perhaps there are two kinds of 4GLs: those for the information center (to be used by users), and those for the development center (to be used by software developers). According to Steven

Bender of Phoenix Software, who provided this insight to Kador, Focus falls into the former category. Perhaps user 4GLs just cannot be expected to do the complex tasks that more powerful 4GLs (such as Ideal and Cygnet) can do.

And in its "Annual CASE Survey 1988," QED Information Sciences and CASE Research Corporation found that although CASE is justified on productivity improvement (nearly 30 percent of CASE users cited that as the prime reason for purchase), it is in quality improvement and communication that the payoff comes. Nearly 25 percent said "improved quality of design" was the top benefit, and nearly 15 percent found both "improved user communication" and "improved developer communication" to be significant benefits.

Putting all of that another way, there is still a lot for us to learn about software automation. The benefits are evolutionary rather than the oft-claimed revolutionary. Perhaps what is appropriate for the user and what is appropriate for the developer are two different things. And certainly quality seems to be more important than productivity in measuring the actual benefits.

What's Wrong with Compiler Writing?

What course does almost every self-respecting computer science degree program offer to upper-level students?

Well, there are probably several answers to that question, but one of them is "compiler writing."

There are several curious things about this fact. One of them is, the world doesn't really need very many compiler-writers. Even for those of us who've had the good luck to work on a compiler project, we realize that we're among the fortunate few. The bulk of the computer world solves application problems. Like recordkeeping, or process control, or engineering calculation. Only a few hardware vendors and software houses actually write compilers.

Even in the micro world, where seemingly every basement turns out a Turbo SNOBOL or a Compact COBOL, the number of successful products is very small. The rest of the would-be compiler-writers eventually have to turn to some other way to make an honest living, like writing payroll programs or selling real estate. Compiler writing, for most of us software folk, is much more of a dream than it is a reality.

There are a couple of reasons, I suppose, why computer science programs continue to teach compiler writing. One is that some occupants of ivy-covered halls simply aren't aware of the realities of software life, and don't know that compiler writing is an uncommon occupation. But more often, compiler writing is taught because the learning experiences of compiler writing, such as text processing and symbol table manipulation, reinforce and enhance skills needed for other applications. If you know how to parse a programming language and store data attributes in a symbol table, then you're well on your way to being able to process sophisticated application input languages, and manipulate data bases. At least, that's the way the theory goes.

But that's not the story I set out to tell here. There's another fact about compiler writing which, considering what we've just talked about, is very surprising.

Compiler writing as an occupation is an economic graveyard. An astounding number of compiler-writing companies flat out don't make it, profitwise. For all the technical preparation of compiler-writers in college, there's something missing when it comes time to apply it in practice.

Want some instances?

- In the 1960s, Computer Sciences Corporation had an unparalleled reputation in compiler writing. Not only were they winning the important commercial contracts, but they had developed two sophisticated and important tools to help do it: GENESYS, a compiler-compiler, and SYMPL, a special-purpose language (now, we'd call it a fourth-generation language) for compiler writing. Yet now, CSC is essentially out of the business. Why? Because at the bottom line, they simply couldn't control the profits well enough.

- At about the same time, System Development Company was another leader in compiler technology. One of their employees, Jules Schwartz, invented and had named after him JOVIAL (Jules' Own Version of the International Algorithmic Language) which until recently was still in use by the Air Force as its standard programming language. The same thing happened to SDC that happened to CSC. They lost money on enough compiler contracts that they decided to turn their talents elsewhere.

- In the 1980s, companies like SofTech and Intermetrics were at the top of the compiler heap, working on apparently lucrative contracts for the Ada programming language. Yet once again, problems arose. SofTech, which had already had some tough times with its most recent JOVIAL compiler contract, got into even more trouble with their Ada effort and eventually the Army, the contracting agent, took the still unfinished compiler and gave it away to any one who wanted it. Intermetrics had some of the same problems. Even experienced contemporary compiler companies are having a hard time succeeding in this difficult business.

- Perhaps the saddest story of all is the one about a little compiler specialty company of the 1960s called Digitek. Digitek had honed some very special compiler-building skills, and like some of the other compiler-building companies of its time had a family of tools to help automate the compiler-writing process. Full of confidence on some early compiler efforts, Digitek tackled a PL/1 contract from a major hardware vendor. And bent their compiler pick. They couldn't control the schedule, couldn't control the budget, and eventually lost control of the company. Digitek went into bankruptcy only a year or two after they appeared to be at the top of the heap among compiler builders. (On the positive side, though, some of the original Digitek founders went on to become Ryan-McFarland, a successful microcomputer compiler company.)

So what's the moral here? Why is compiler writing, taught to so many computer science students over the years, so badly understood?

My theory goes something like this.

There are two problems here.

The first is academic naivete. Compiler writing, in the world of professional compiler construction, is a lot more than parsing and symbol tables. There's selection of object code sequences, register optimization, program flow analysis, and even the mundane task of diagnostic production. And all of that adds up to a more complex package than the third-year CSci student ever dreamed of.

Then there's the second reason. It's what I call the onion theory of application problems. The more layers there are to the problem, the more rapidly the solution to the problem escalates in complexity. The academic exercise of building an unoptimized compiler for a Pascal subset is a lot different from the professional task of building a full COBOL compiler and its libraries. And, perhaps more to the point, the professional task of building a full Fortran compiler still doesn't prepare the compiler builder for the complexities of an Ada compiler. The bigger the language, the more exponentially grows the compiler. And the harder it becomes to control the schedule and the budget. And from there, the harder it becomes to make money building compilers. And at the bottom line, the harder it becomes to stay in the compiler business.

Compiler building also has limited interest, for the same reason that teaching compiler writing is questionable. There just aren't enough readers out there with enough of a need-to-know to care. But there are some interesting and general learning experiences, nevertheless.

One is that the correlation between what we as a society teach and what the learners need to learn is a tenuous one at best. And that goes as much for courses in operating systems and data bases as it does for compiler writing.

The other is that control of complexity is vitally important to technology (we all knew that already), but it's also vitally important to economics. And that's a sobering thought as we enter yet another era of ever larger and more complicated computing undertakings.

That's not to say we software folks can't handle complexity. But in a business where the shakeout rate is analogous to the auto company failure rate of the 1920s and 1930s, understanding the role of complexity may well make the difference between the winners and the losers.

And ten years from now, we'd all sure prefer to be among the winners!

High-Order Language: How High is Up?

A high-order language is a programming language closer to the application domain than to the machine domain. (Stay with me, now. I know there was nothing new in what I just said, but I want to take you toward some new thoughts.)

An assembler language, by that definition (and to the surprise of none of us), is *not* high order because it is nearly the same language that the computer executes. Pascal and Ada and COBOL are high-order languages because the computer cannot execute them without help from an elaborate compiler or interpreter.

Ultimately, an application program which has an input language by means of which the user communicates goals to the program is the highest-level language of all.

Thus, languages span a spectrum, ranging from machine code at the lowest level to application-specific languages at the highest level.

We software people rarely think of languages this way. Languages to us are things programmers use, and users feeding data into an application program are doing something else. But that distinction is getting blurred now and deservedly so. Application programs have ever more sophisticated user interfaces, some of them even having "languages" which the user can "program." Some 4GLs are designed with the idea that users can program in them. It is the goal of a great deal of computer science research and a great deal of user political power to transition some of the programmer's traditional domain into the user's domain. Inevitably, this means new kinds of languages which don't need programmers to program them.

There are a couple of ways we software people can respond to this trend. One is to wring our hands about the erosion of our turf, and either give up or mount a war to hold tightly to what we have "always" had.

But there is another way. As responsible technical people, we can acknowledge that users are sometimes best equipped to solve their own problems, and help them by providing ever more powerful user facilities. And we can acknowledge that in general it is technically desirable to solve a problem in the highest language possible, even if that means using off-the-shelf solutions instead of writing new code.

A couple of years ago, that last sentence might have been just another piece of Motherhood. But in the 1990s, with an incredible number of new-concept components emerging from an astoundingly creative software marketplace, there are a lot more choices on the shelf than you might ever have dreamed. Have you looked at what a Macintosh will do for you with little or no programming effort, for example? There is a new world opening up out there.

So let's look a little more deeply at the philosophy behind the spectrum of solution languages available to the programmer and his or her partner, the user, to see what kinds of decisions this year's technologist might make.

In general, productivity and quality are increased by using the highest-level language consistent with the problem to be solved. For example, if an off-the-shelf application solution is already available (and presuming it possesses reasonably strong quality attributes), then that is the best solution to the problem.

If, stepping down one level because we struck out at the higher level, a fourth-generation language (4GL) is available which addresses the problem, then it should be used. That may mean having a programmer do the programming, or having a user to do the programming, depending on which 4GL and which application are being considered. (4GLs are usually focused on commercial data processing applications, especially those involving data base use.)

Exhausting those possibilities, then a good traditional programming language (e.g., Modula 2 or Fortran or COBOL or . . .) should be chosen.

And finally, if all else fails, then a machine or assembly level solution must be used.

What are the factors which drive us down the chain of choice from highest to lowest?

Capability is one. Highest-level languages are often narrowly focused on a very specific problem and may not be useful for the presumably new problem at hand.

Efficiency is another. Generally there is a loss of computer resource efficiency as we move up the language levels, and sometimes that loss may be intolerable at the highest level.

Each of the quality attributes (portability, reliability, efficiency, human engineering, testability, understandability, and modifiability), in fact, must be evaluated against the proposed level of solution to ensure that the reduced price of a cheaper programming solution up front is not more than paid for in time by a lower-quality solution.

The benefits of the highest possible language level are many:

- Productivity is improved, often dramatically.
- High-order languages finesse whole levels of solution effort, eliminating chances for error. For example, assembler level programmers must manipulate hardware-specific registers, and run the risk of making many register allocation errors. It is not possible for a higher-level language programmer to make register errors, because the programmer cannot and does not need to access registers.
- There are fewer lines of code in a high-level solution, and thus fewer chances for errors.
- Structured code is facilitated by a high-level languages. Interestingly, in the highest-level solutions the code may not even need to be structured since it can be presented to the computer in a nonprocedural way (order of execution is a function of the language processor, not the programmer).
- Portability is facilitated by the higher-level languages.
- Maintainability is facilitated by the higher-level languages.
- Testability is facilitated by the higher-level languages.

In essence, what we are saying here is that most of the quality attributes are made better by the highest-level language solution possible. As we mentioned before, efficiency is a counterexample, and problems which need an extremely efficient solution will find themselves moving down the language level chain until the best compromise between the needed quality attributes can be obtained.

It is not often that productivity and quality walk hand in hand. Using the highest-level language possible, you have a good chance of making it happen.

Should We Prepare for a 4GL Future?

Some say 4GLs are magic and that with them, a revolution is under way in our ability to build software. Others say 4GLs are oversold and that with them (when they apply to the task at hand) productivity improvements can be made. The trouble is, these people say, they often don't apply to the task at hand.

If the first set of people are right, then every programmer in the world ought to be learning about 4GLs. If the second set of people are right, then those programmers whose application domains can be helped by 4GLs should be learning about them. Either way, then, the issue of training and education about 4GLs is important.

The use of two distinct terms—*training* and *education*—was intentional in the last paragraph. It is a distinction that will become even more important as this essay progresses. Training, as we use the term, is learning with an immediate payoff. Education, as we use it, is learning with a longer-term payoff. Companies offer "training" courses in how to use a particular software product, such as a word processor or a new language compiler. Colleges and universities offer "education" courses in more general concepts, such as text processing or programming languages.

If learning about 4GLs is important, who should be responsible for providing that learning experience? Training, almost everyone agrees, is industry's job. Education, by the same token, is generally the task of the academic world. Are the training and education people actually providing the approaches to 4GLs that the world needs? Now the plot thickens.

There are plenty of training courses available, usually in the use of a particular 4GL and provided by the vendor of the 4GL. So, for openers, it is certainly possible to say that the training needs are readily satisfied.

But education is another story. Most colleges and universities don't talk about 4GLs. The reason why they don't, and even the question of whether they do or not, is the subject of some controversy.

The Problem

That controversy boiled to a head when an interview with James Martin, leading proponent of 4GLs, was published by *Communications of the ACM* in March 1985. Academia, said Martin, is not doing its job in educating people about the magic of 4GLs. Yes we are, said several academics who participated in a teleconference with Martin on the subject.

The Posturing

Reaching an agreement on the problem is obscured by several factors, not the least of which is the emotional climate which has come to settle around the subject of 4GLs. Proponents make claims rivaling those of patent medicine salespeople. Opponents, seemingly driven to the opposite extreme, ignore the claims and the products, behaving as if they were useless. In this emotional milieu, posturing to support a position becomes commonplace.

For example, in the Martin interview and teleconference, one proponent of 4GLs said, early in the interview, "in most companies, nobody has done anything" with 4GLs. Later, in the heat of battle, the same person said "most DP installations today use" 4GLs.

The opponents of 4GLs are nearly as bad. On the defensive, one academic said "some universities are teaching squarely in the center" of 4GL technology. But when pressed for specifics, the same person admitted that 4GLs are one of several topics which may be "considered" in "graduate seminars," hardly the mainstream of computer science education.

The Positions

It is easy to state the position of the 4GL proponent on this issue: The 4GL is too important, they say, to be omitted from the educational program. To the extent that colleges and universities ignore it, they are not keeping pace with new technology. To the extent that the technology is slow to migrate into the industrial setting, it is partly the fault of academia for failing to highlight its importance.

The position of the 4GL opponent, or those few who are neutral on 4GLs, is a little harder to state: The 4GL is not as important as its advocates claim, they would say for openers. We must be careful not to degenerate into training instead of education, they would say as a follow-on, and 4GL coursework comes awfully close to the former.

There is another reason for the disinterest in academia, and it is not nearly as philosophical as the first two reasons. There is a price tag attached to 4GL technology—language processors and support tools are very expensive—and most academic institutions have a hard time justifying high-cost educational add-ons.

But all this discussion still avoids one other key factor in the 4GL education controversy. Computer science education, as it is currently taught, studiously avoids much of the data processing community. And 4GLs as we currently know them are of most value to just this community. "The graduates from the best departments are not going to work for the large banks and insurance companies, as much as they're going to work for the computer manufacturers," said one academic. There is a "tension between the DP industry and computer science departments," said another, and "near the root of the problem is the lack of resources for computer science."

In other words, the whole 4GL education dilemma is piggybacked on top of two larger problems, the lack of computer science attention to data processing and the lack of resources for teaching computer science properly, and it is unlikely to get solved as long as the blocking problems remain in the way.

Toward a Solution

Is it possible to begin chiseling away at the problem of 4GL education in spite of this dilemma?

A couple of things can help. One is for the proponents of 4GLs to recognize the dilemma, its blocking factors, and to begin isolating those 4GL factors which are education and not training. One proponent began that process in the interview, identifying some of the principles which need to accompany 4GL education:

- automatic navigation in data base systems
- the ability to generate code without conventional programming
- nonprocedural constructs
- graphics workbench tools for analysts

These are clearly not training issues, and thus are a large step toward an underlying body of educational knowledge for 4GLs. But they are also still fuzzy concepts and need to be fleshed out into teachable ideas.

Also helpful would be for computer science academics to realize that they are bound, with good reason, to standard definitions of curricula, but that this binding may inhibit their ability to respond when truly exciting new technology really does arrive. It is vital for the CSci community and its curriculum people to provide for the possibility of rapid change in the technology, just as a configuration management organization, while promoting stability by inhibiting change, must have emergency processes for overriding this basic conservatism.

Conclusion

It is difficult to talk about how important 4GLs are, and how important training and education in them is. But as we approach the issue, we see other problems standing in the way whose resolution is at least as important as the 4GL dilemma which brought them to our attention.

Do we really intend that data processing and its needs be separated from computer science as some sort of unworthy stepchild? Do we really intend that computer science be so bound to its now traditional curriculum concepts that it is unable to adjust to new and important concepts which emerge from industrial uses of computing?

There may be a connection between a "yes" answer to these questions and computer science's inability to attract the funding needed to keep it at the forefront of the computing profession.

What's Really Wrong with Cobol?

Name the world's most popular programming languages in terms of use. What would you come up with?

The latest idea I've seen would show COBOL at the top, with a world-beating lead over its competitors. Down the line somewhere would come either RPG or Fortran, depending on whose data you were looking at. After that would come Pascal, and beyond that the numbers dwindle to nothingness fairly rapidly.

Now contrast that with a list of those languages computer scientists see as good. Whatever you would care to put at the top, my guess is that it's not anywhere visible on the popularity list. Modula II? Ada? LISP? Prolog? You'll find very little practical support for the value of these languages.

Let's think about that a little bit. Sure, COBOL and RPG and Fortran all have flaws. Sure, Modula II and Pascal and Ada are serious attempts to correct those flaws. So why is there such a dichotomy between what gets used and what gets touted?

Well, there's the old notion of entrenchment. The older, flawed languages have been around and in use so long that people can't afford to quit using them. There's a lot of truth to that.

But there's something else happening here, too. With all that heavy use of COBOL in the business world, where money is to be made by cutting costs wherever possible, why haven't at least a few companies switched to something better? No, I don't mean 4GLs. I mean 3GLs that provide the same capabilities as COBOL. Why haven't the innovative, advanced firms started using a better COBOL?

Here's where I want to get to the real point of this essay. I want to take the position that people aren't switching away from COBOL because there really isn't anything better to switch to.

Heresy! Ignorance! Stupidity! I can hear the silent cries from my reading audience now. But wait, there is method in my madness, and I would like to explain.

First of all, let me take another position. A programming language is a tool, and its sole reason for being is to provide a means of expressing the solution to a computer-solvable problem.

With that statement, I want to reject the claims that the best language is the one with the most new features. If the new features don't assist in solving my particular problem, then I would assert they are an interesting novelty but not a valuable addition to my toolkit.

With that in mind, let us look at the application domain for which COBOL was designed. It is a data-oriented, file-oriented world, characterized by record-structured data, fixed-length character string motion, and edited report generation. That's an oversimplification, of course, but it's a good starting point from which to go back and look at the notion of languages as tools. What other tools have been invented to address this problem domain?

Nominate Pascal or Modula II or Ada if you will, but if you are honest with yourself you will find sufficient clumsiness in force-fitting those languages to the business application domain and you will soon come to realize that there must be a better way.

That better way is still COBOL. That's the gist of my heresy.

Does that mean I think COBOL is a good language? Emphatically, my answer is a resounding "No."

The world needs a better COBOL. It has needed a better COBOL for nearly a quarter of a century now. COBOL is verbose, it resists structuring, it is difficult to make modular, . . . the list goes on.

But COBOL does satisfy the requirements of its application domain. It has special features which make it simple to do each of the major tasks which characterize that domain. No more modern language does those things as well.

Why? Why is this ancient and clumsy language not replaced by something that does its job more cleanly? Because, I would assert, the research world which might create a better language is so disdainful of business application software in general, and the COBOL language in particular, that it is blind to the thought that a major research challenge lies in defining a better COBOL.

I suggest that a computer science researcher, who is looking for a new and better road to software productivity, take a long look at the COBOL world. I also suggest that researcher gather the requirements which underlie a language for that world and design a language that meets those requirements, using some of the better language concepts that have come along since the origin of COBOL in the 1950s. Finally the researcher should publish his or her findings so that the marketplace of new ideas can ascertain their value.

In the 1970s some computer people were saying such things as "COBOL will no longer be in use by 1980" and "COBOL is hopeless." Obviously, COBOL has outlived the predictions of those naysayers. Not because it deserved to. After all, to paraphrase Churchill, "COBOL is a very bad language—but the others are so much worse."

A researcher unafraid of working in the mundane world of busines data processing *could* make those earlier predictions come true. And do a fascinating job of research work at the same time.

Do you know anyone who'd like to try?

Achieving Greatness
in the Software World

Greatness is an elusive thing.

Partly because not many people have the stuff it takes to achieve greatness. But also because greatness depends on timing as well as the right stuff.

Take, for instance, greatness in the software world. If you achieved greatness in the early years of the software field, you did it with an entirely different set of personal qualities than those it would take now. Let me make that statement come alive with three partly fictionalized stories about three great software people—all different from each other, all products of their era.

Back in 1958, Woody Codalot was a household name among programming people. How did Woody get his fame? By implementing some of the best general purpose software known to man—the stuff that nowadays we would call "software parts," the software that other programmers plug into their own code so that they won't have to do what we have forever called "reinvent the wheel."

Woody wrote one of the earliest operating systems, a primitive-for-now but elegant-then package which freed programmers from needing to

119

get tangled up with the hardware intimacies that operating systems people need to understand. And Woody also wrote a lot of smaller-scale but still valuable support software—random number generators, and trigonometric functions, and stuff like that—you know the kind.

Did Woody get rich from all this activity? Well, no. It may be difficult for you to believe this, but back in those days software was free! It hadn't occurred to anyone yet that software was anything other than what you gave away with hardware in order to be able to sell the hardware. And Woody's greatness was achieved by contributing his software to an organization called *Share*, an IBM user group whose role in life was to make software written by one user company available to others. (If you've been to a Share meeting lately, you'll notice how far the organization has strayed from its original mold!) Woody's greatness was achieved because (1) his name was on a lot of software listed in the *Share* manual (now we'd call it a software parts catalog), and (2) everyone had come to learn that if Woody did it, it was good software. You couldn't call yourself a programmer and not have heard of Woody Codalot.

A decade and a half later, in 1973, no one remembered Woody Codalot. There were new names and new mechanisms for gaining fame in the software world. One of the best known was Wolfgang Writalot. How did Wolfgang get his fame? By doing software research and publishing papers on his findings. What kind of research, and what kind of papers?

Well, perhaps you remember the early years of the structured programming revolution. Wolfgang was one of those whose studies resulted in his advocating careful structure and the attendant minimization of GOTOs in programs. His findings were published in the Association for Software Professional's journal *Transactions and Communications*, and eventually ended up reprinted in several books on structured programming. He also lectured frequently on the subject, and his name appeared ever more frequently as a speaker and perhaps even keynoter at computing conferences. If you knew anything about structured programming, you knew about Wolfgang.

Now Woody Codalot, as we saw, was a practicing software professional. As a matter of fact, he worked in industry for Wings Aloft Aviation. Contrast that with Wolfgang Writalot, who was a researcher and professor at a leading computer-science school, Ivyclad College. The way to greatness had made an enormous transition in the intervening decade, from doing it to thinking about doing it.

And that brings us to our third great software person, Gates Sellalot. In 1984, the software world had completed a dramatic shift that had begun many years before. Remember that in Woody Codalot's time software was free? Well, by the time Gates Sellalot came along, that day was gone forever. Not only was software no longer free, there were fortunes to be made in it. And Gates Sellalot was right in there with the best of them.

Gates, a few years before in his happy hacker days, had conceived of a new idea in report generation programs which eventually came to be known as the spreadsheet program. He developed his spreadsheet, and then he enhanced it, and then he enhanced it some more. But after a while, he got tired of the technology of enhancements, and decided to see how well he could do as a huckster of software—how many people would really want to buy a copy of his spreadsheet? The answer, as you well know by now, was staggering. It was in the hundreds of thousands, if not in the millions. And suddenly, software was big business. Gates Sellalot, looking a lot like Horatio Alger, was on the cover of Everyman's magazine, along with the magazine's announcement that software was man of the year, just as the computer had been two years before.

And Gates was a millionaire. He was president of his own company, an acknowledged successful manager as well as technologist, and his name was a household word throughout the world. Now *that's* greatness!

Let's take another look at where we've been, here. Woody Codalot was great because he was a master at technology. Wolfgang Writalot was great because he was a master at theory. And Gates Sellalot was great because he was a master of marketing. Create an idea, revise the idea through careful study, and sell the idea. Perhaps these three people as individuals didn't have a lot in common; but perhaps there's a software-independent progression here, and perhaps it's somewhere at the heart of our capitalistic system.

There's just one more thing I want to say about greatness. Think back over the great people we know about. Pull a name out at random. How about Abraham Lincoln. What made him great?

Well, he kept the Union together and he freed the slaves. But how did he do it? Put yourself back in time to the early 1860s, and imagine youself trying to make the decision that Abraham Lincoln had to make. Do you go to war to hold the Union together, or do you let it come unglued? (Remember, freeing the slaves was sort of an afterthought which came up later).

Especially in our antiwar era, my suspicion is that, if you're truly honest with yourself, you'll have a tough time deciding. And it won't help much if you look at the casualty figures for the Civil War. Holding the Union together took a staggering toll in human lives. The choice Lincoln made, then, was a difficult and perhaps even arbitrary one.

And, more to the point, I would assert that it was not his decision that made Lincoln great. It was that, once having made the decision, he made sure that his decision looked to history like the right one. And he did that by putting all his energies into winning the war. If the North had lost the war, would Lincoln have been perceived as great? No, I suspect he'd have been cast by history just like Jefferson Davis . . . an also-ran, perhaps even looked down upon, in the annals of history.

But that's a philosophical digression. Let's return to the subject of software greatness.

Want to play a game? Think about this question.

What'll it take to achieve greatness in the software world during the next decade? Will it be technology? Theory? Marketing? Or something entirely new? If you can play this game well enough, the next great person in software might be you!

A New Way of Looking
at Software Productivity

How can we improve software productivity by orders of magnitude?

That was a question the Department of Defense asked a few years ago. It's a question all of us in the computing profession have asked ourselves over the years, for that matter.

There tend to be two kinds of people who respond to that question. One kind, those who think they know how we can do software 10 or 100 times better, propose to do it with lots of research money and methodology breakthroughs. "Give us X thousand dollars," these people say, "and we will show you how to do automatic code generation from problems posed by experts on cocktail napkins."

The other kind of persons, those who think that no one knows how to do software 10 or 100 times better, wring their hands and say things like "Alas, don't throw any more money after that problem, it appears to be unsolvable."

Like so many other polarized life situations, hardly anyone is taking a middle ground between these two extremes. Is there any combination of currently known techniques which can lead to significant improvement in software productivity? Only a few people are exploring that question, let alone tentatively offering a "yes" answer.

Of course, there are the methodology hucksters who promise those kinds of improvements from whatever they happen to be selling at the moment, usually a technique called something like "Structured Poobah." It's been hard to discuss the matter rationally with those folks, because they're so busy selling that they haven't time to talk about the existence of any hard evidence to support their claims.

There is, however, some disquieting data on that subject. One set, visibly enough, is found on the cover of Barry Boehm's book, *Software Engineering Economics*. Boehm's data show that, when it comes to productivity, methodologies and languages and other technology approaches are down in the noise level of improvements.

A few years ago an article appeared in one of the professional journals which reported the results of exploring experimental research findings on the benefits of methodology improvements, such as the structured methodologies. The conclusion of the study was that no experiments existed which could shed any significant light on their benefits. That was kind of a downer!

At a more recent computing conference, researchers reported on one small experiment into one small area, the benefit of using structured versus unstructured code. In this experiment, the benefits were clear (that was the good news) but nominal (that was the bad news)—down around 5 percent.

At that rate, it would take quite a collection of methodologies to add up to an order of magnitude improvement. Looked at realistically, these data indicate that we may not get there from here that way.

But let's look at the cover of Boehm's book once again. There *was* one productivity factor which was head and shoulders above the rest. It was the *quality of the people* doing the software work. Perhaps here, in the sociology of the technology of the software field, is the answer to the DoD's question.

Are good people orders of magnitude better than the others at developing software? There's been a steady trickle of experiential and experimental data on that subject over the past 20 years. And the answer is a fairly solid *yes*—the data show that good people do various software tasks 7 to 28 *times* better than the others.

Well, then, if people are one of the keys to productivity, what can we do about it? Could we, for example, find out what the good people do? And once we found out, could we transfer that technology to the others?

There are, now and at long last, some people who are exploring those questions. They call the field "empirical studies of programming."

The chief motivators of the movement are people like Elliot Soloway of the University of Michigan, Bill Curtis of the MCC, and Ben Shneiderman of the University of Maryland. There's a lot of enthusiasm among these pioneers, and there is also the beginning of some solid and useful results.

What kind of results? Well, let's take an analytical look at three papers presented at three different places which reported on experiments pursuing this goal. One paper, "Problem Solving for Effective Systems Analysis: An Experimental Exploration" (*Communications of the ACM*, November 1983, by Vitalari and Dickson) reported on a look at requirements generation by "good" versus "less good" professional systems analysts.

Another paper, "You Can Observe a Lot Just Watching How Designers Design" (*Proceedings of the Eighth Annual NASA Goddard Software Workshop*, November 1983, by Littman, Ehrlich, Soloway, and Black) reported on a look at "experienced" versus "inexperienced" designers.

The third paper, "Why Software Maintenance is Hard" (the findings were reported in various places including *Systems Development*, August 1985, by Soloway) discussed "expert" versus "novice" software maintainers.

Surprisingly, there were common threads in these papers. Listen, now, this may be important. Good/experienced/expert people did several discernible things that their lesser counterparts did not do. What were they?

1. They set more goals, more subgoals, and they worked top-down from the goals.
2. They looked for analogies to prior problems, and set up models based on those analogies.
3. They were more systematic. They verbalized more strategies, keeping notes on assumptions and constraints and expectations. They specified a less ambiguous final product (e.g., systems analysts specified more requirements).
4. They tried and rejected more hypotheses. They modified more strategies.
5. They were more people oriented in some ways. The systems analysts facilitated better user relationships. The maintainers analyzed the stylistic quality of the development programmers who originally built the code, relating the people to the code.

Fair enough, that's an interesting list. Across three disciplines as diverse as systems analysis/design/maintenance, that's even fairly surprising. But so what?

Well, what if we could transfer that technology? What if we could educate programmers to do such things as working with goals, or using analogies? What if we freed up software developers to be willing to try and reject more hypotheses? (The achievement of brilliance, we need to learn, is often iterative and littered with failure, rather than instantaneous.) What if we explored the other answers in this short list, and the other answers the empirical studies people are beginning to come up with?

Then, could we achieve orders of magnitude improvement in software productivity?

It's worth exploring.

Productivity and Theory G

Everybody else is talking about productivity. Why shouldn't I?

After all, it was the hot button topic of the 1980s. Somehow, by a magical process that I still don't understand, the year 1979 was torn off calendars all over the country and the tearers immediately muttered to themselves, "Productivity—that's where it's at."

Was it printed there in invisible ink by calendar manufacturers? As we approached 1984, were we being mass telecommunicated to without our knowledge? How did all of those speakers get all of that material from which to start presenting all of those expert opinions on the same subject in the same time frame?

The only thing that I can think of that's like it is the age-level-strata communication system we all pass through. Perhaps you haven't recognized that phenomenon yet. Here is what I mean:

There's a communication flow which occurs at the third-grade level, and information is passed on from last year's third grader to this year's third grader, without either the parent system or the teacher system getting into the act. For example, every third grader knows that a country which has nothing but pink cars is a pink carnation. Now, did we tell them that?

Would the teachers tell them that? Of course not, only a child would tell another child such a bad, third-grade level joke.

Take another example. Those of us who are approaching middle age (incidentally, no one ever reaches middle age, we simply approach it) remember an old saying which included the phrase "Catch an (ethnic slur) by his toe." Would you believe that the kids of today, to a little person, don't know that saying? What they know is "Catch a *tiger* by his toe." How did they all learn that? How did the offensive version die out? By the same kind of third-grade level communication flow mechanism. I don't understand it, but it's there. And it's there at other age levels, too. And, to return to my point, perhaps it's there at the professional level, as well—a pipeline that pulses through us all forming the phrase "productivity" over and over again.

Be that as it may, here it is the 1990s and here am I, feeling compelled to discuss productivity. What I want to tell you about is Productivity Theory G. Theory G is my own personal theory about productivity. (Note the clever relationship between the letter G and the first letter of my last name!). And Theory G, to shorten a long story, contains these components:

Subtheory G11:   A system built on adversary relationships is rarely subject to significant compromise.

Subtheory G12:   The American labor system is built on a labor-management adversary relationship.

Subtheory G13:   Worthwhile productivity improvement must involve significant compromise.

This leads us to:

Theory G1:   Worthwhile productivity improvement is nearly impossible in the American labor system as it currently exists.

Proof of Theory G1:   Look at the British system. Labor and management are impossibly stalemated. British productivity stagnates. Q.E.D.

Subtheory G21:   Where labor-management adversaries are not clearly defined, productivity improvements are still possible.

Subtheory G22:   Computing is too new for labor-management adversary relationships to be well formed.

Theory G2:   Productivity improvements involving the development of, and perhaps the use of, computers are still possible.

Proof of Theory G2:   I am not in a union. You are probably not in a union. My management still listens to me, sometimes. Probably yours does, too. Labor-management cooperation is more common than labor-management confrontation, where we are.

Subtheory G31:   Motivation is an important part of productivity improvement.

Subtheory G32:   Computing management more often espouses control than motivation.

Theory G3:   Computing management is veering in the direction of destroying what chance for productivity improvement it still has.

Proof of Theory G3:   Do you enjoy going to work as much as you did five years ago? I suspect not.

Overall Theory G: It may be too late for the American system to gain major productivity improvement. Computing still holds out hope. Computing management may destroy that hope.

Well, there's my Theory G on productivity. Sorry about the seriousness, there. I guess whatever it was that told me I had to talk about productivity also told me that productivity couldn't be treated lightly. But at least I sugarcoated the pill.

Barry Boehm's "Theory W" Principle of Software Project Management

What can software managers do to improve software productivity?

There are lots of answers to that question. But Dr. Barry W. Boehm of TRW has come up with a new one. He calls it "Theory W Software Management."

Why Theory W? Well, there's already a Theory X, a Theory Y, and a Theory Z (see box). Why not a Theory W to continue the alphabetic progression ?!

What does the W in Theory W mean? It stands for "make everyone a Winner." That is, do everything you can to make all the players in a software project (the managers, the customers, the users, the developers and the maintainers) have a "win" in the resulting product. By a "win," Boehm means that each player has achieved most or all of their goals for and about the project.

Boehm describes the steps toward achieving Theory W as

1. Establish a set of win-win preconditions. Understand what the win conditions for each player really are. Establish objectives which in-

clude making those wins possible. Provide a supportive environment in which all participants accept the possibility of a win-win solution.

2. Structure a win-win software process. Establish a realistic process plan, including the flagging of win-lose and lose-lose situations as risks. Provide feedback which keeps the players involved as negotiation and compromise proceed.

3. Structure a win-win software product. Define a final software product which matches all the win conditions, particularly those of the user and the maintainer.

Typical win conditions for the various players in a software project are:

- Management wants the product built with no overruns and no surprises.
- Customers want the project built as quickly as possible within budget.
- Users want lots of functions, a fast and robust product, and user-friendliness.
- Developers want an interesting career path, a project built with integrity, and the minimization of documentation writing.
- Maintainers want a bug-free product, good documentation, and a product that is easy to change.

It is not always easy to meet all of these sometimes conflicting goals. And in addition to that, each of the players as individuals probably has goals which will help identify what a "win" is to them. A win-win solution, Boehm points out, must be negotiated in both functional terms (the preceding list) and personal terms.

The opposite of a win-win product, Boehm says, include quick, cheap, and sloppy products which result in a "win" for the developer and the customer but a "lose" for the user; a product with lots of bells and whistles which results in a "win" for the developer and user but a "lose" for the customer; or a product resulting from driving a hard bargain, where the "win" is for the customer and user but the developers lose. Boehm points out that, in these situations, no one really wins.

The Theory W approach, as can be seen from the preceding diverse and conflicting goals, is harder to apply than it might at first appear. Boehm points out that data processing professionals, whose social needs relative to growth needs are far lower than most other professionals, find it hard to seek solutions in people terms. Boehm recommends a four-step approach to solving this problem:

1. Separate the people from the problem.
2. Focus on interests, not positions.

3. Invent options for mutual gain.

4. Insist on using objective criteria to analyze the results.

There are several criteria which must be met if a software management theory is to be effective, Boehm says. It must be simple, it must be general, and it must be specific.

Simplicity means that the theory can be expressed concisely, and yet detailed guidelines can be derived from the basic concept. Theory W, Boehm says, satisfies this goal since it is expressed in four words and three steps.

Generality means that the theory must apply to all classes of products. Theory W has no application domain dependencies.

Specificity means that the theory can be applied directly to a particular project with a clear-cut method of approach and with criteria for testing the result. Boehm has applied the theory in several specific projects.

Any software management theory must also provide a basis for the framework of management activities. Boehm cited the Koontz-O'Donnell management framework, which contains five processses: planning, organizing, staffing, directing, and controlling. Boehm points out that Theory W can be useful in each of these activities.

SOME OTHER PROJECT MANAGEMENT THEORIES AND THEIR APPLICATION TO SOFTWARE

What are the other commonly advocated management theories? Dr. Barry Boehm identifies three: Theory X, Theory Y, and Theory Z.

Theory X:

- People inherently dislike work.
- They have to be coerced into working.
- They prefer being told what to do.

Theory Y:

- People don't inherently dislike work.
- People can exercise self-direction.
- Commitment to objectives depends on resulting rewards.
- People can learn to seek responsibility.
- Work creativity is widely distributed.
- People potential is only partly utilized.

Theory Z:

- People work best toward goals which they have helped establish.
- Once people have bought into goals, you can trust them to perform.
- If people share a common set of values, they can develop workable project goals.

According to Boehm, there are problems in applying each of these three theories to software management. Theory X is based on an assumption that people must be prodded into doing work; this tends to result in an adversarial management-developer relationship, and in fact does not accurately reflect the nature of software people. Theory Y is based on an assumption that people will work well if they are rewarded properly; this tends to result in the creation of a self-oriented work force, and tends to break down when conflict is encountered. Theory Z, the so-called "Japanese-style management," is useful in a single community of workers, but tends to break down when multiple organizations, such as software's managers, customers, users, developers, and maintainers are involved.

Interestingly, Boehm also points out some problems in applying another famous human relations dictum, the Golden Rule. "Do unto others as you would have others do unto you," Boehm points out, is usually interpreted by software people as "Do unto others as you would have others do unto you—if you were like them." But software people have different goals from, say, customers and users, and this interpretation of the Golden Rule simply will not work, Boehm says.

Software
Productivity Improvement:
Who's Doing What?

What if you had a few million dollars, and you had a burning desire to attack the software productivity problem? What would you do?

There are three answers to that question already in existence, as it turns out. Three different organizations were established in the last decade to try to accelerate the state of the practice in software.

First came the Microelectronics and Computer Technology Consortium (MCC), founded in 1983 by 12 computer and software companies, in Austin, Texas. Then came the Software Engineering Institute (SEI), founded in 1984 by the U.S. Department of Defense, in Pittsburgh. And finally came the Software Productivity Consortium (SPC), founded in 1985 by 14 aerospace companies, located in Reston, Virginia.

Each of the three was established to advance the state of the art in computer technology. And each is going about it in a rather different way!

The giant of the three, MCC, is also the most diverse. Around 400 people are employed there, but less than 100 are exploring software technology. The goal of the MCC? To develop future technology through research, not to develop products.

SEI, which historically came in second, is also the second largest organization. There are about 150 people, and all are focused on software, but in different areas. For example, one of the early successful arms of the SEI developed software engineering curriculum materials which could be used to teach software engineering topics in academe or in industry. Other areas include developing standards of excellence, serving as a clearing-house for technology information, producing a showcase environment, and analyzing and improving software process.

A third direction has been chosen by the SPC. The 100 or so employees there are specifically dedicated to developing software packages and complete products for common use by their client companies.

So we have one group doing research and not products, a second focusing on accelerating and promulgating knowledge, and a third developing products but not necessarily doing research! Three different directions, indeed!

Two of the three had to overcome an interesting problem. Cooperative ventures of this kind between companies have been frowned on in the past for antitrust reasons. So some new national antitrust legislation was created to pave the way for this new approach.

How do these consortia work? At both the MCC and SPC, the member companies are each represented on the board of directors and, in addition, each contributes technically skilled people to the consortium.

The government-funded SEI, on the other hand, had no antitrust problems. However, its staffing situation is somewhat like that of the other two, since it augments permanent employees with affiliates from academic or industrial organizations which have chosen to participate with the DoD in SEI's progress.

Now, were any of those organizations what you had in mind as an approach for the few million dollars that you intended to put into the problem? If not, there's the possibility of one more model to look at.

This one is only in the thinking stages, so it will go nameless and location-less. But it's a totally different approach from the other three, because it's strictly academically based.

Traditionally, academic institutions have an education component, perhaps a research component, and sometimes a community service component. It is this latter component that is being explored in this new approach.

What constitutes a community service component? Well, consider the continuing education arm of many universities, where classes for community benefit are developed and offered. Or, more to the point, consider the agricultural extension service agent, who takes the knowledge gained in the university research laboratories and carries it out in the field to offer it to the farmers.

Here we have a clear case of an academic institution stimulating productivity. Why not do it in software? Why couldn't an academic institution offer, as a service to its local community or its state, ways to spread research knowledge to the software practitioner?

How could it offer that service? One way could include software agents, assigned to and working with practitioners to explore the practicality of transitioning research into practice. Another way could include providing education to software students, where the education focuses on bridges *between* research and practice, not just on research or on practice as is more commonly done now.

Such a program could most readily be constructed in an innovative academic institution near a center of software activity. It would need a physical place, staff dedicated to this new mission, direct involvement and funding from researchers and practitioners, and a rich, diverse, and supportive traditional academic program.

Could it happen? There are those who are working as this is being written to pull it off. Many of the ideas presented here are in fact from those people.

So there we have four models for an organization to improve software productivity. Two of them are industry based. One is government based. And the last is academia based. It looks like lots of people in this country really care about software productivity improvement.

Software Metrics:
Of Lightning Rods and
Built-up Tension

The speaker on software metrics had just finished his presentation. "Are there any questions?" he asked of the audience.

In the back of the room, a hand went up. From the tone of voice, you could sense immediately that the question was hostile.

"Why do you talk about Halstead metrics?" the questioner asked. "They have been pretty well discredited. They simply don't validate in any meaningful way."

"In fact," the questioner added as if in afterthought, "talking about Halstead's Software Science is about like teaching alchemy in a college course on chemistry."

The room took on a stunned silence. That kind of direct confrontation is rare in technical circles. While the speaker fought both for composure and for an answer to the challenge, I thought about what was happening.

Software metrics, as you probably know, is about the measurement of things pertaining to software. The most famous measurements are about complexity of software. Some other measurements have to do with productivity, and quality, and estimation, and a lot of other things we software folk wish we knew more about. Software metrics is that corner of the software world that seeks quantized answers to what so far have been qualitative issues.

When people talk about software metrics, there are a lot of schools of thought. One of those schools of thought is the Halstead school, the school labeled "software science," the one where basic measures of software are undertaken in order to form a unified theoretical approach to the measurement of the artifacts of software.

It seemed like a good idea when Halstead first came up with it. But over the years, software researchers and developers trying to validate the metrics have encountered more and more frustration. The metric results are sometimes sensitive to the items measured. Many have given up on the value of the work.

But while that has been happening, entrepreneurs have discovered metrics. There are now commercially available tools which caluclate a variety of metrics, including Halstead's, and tout those metrics as the answer to management's plea for knowledge and control of the software development process. Those claims have escalated the emotional setting in which metrics already found itself.

The explosive scene where the speaker was challenged by hostile questions is not atypical of this era's reaction to software metrics. As the speaker regained his composure and began responding as best he could, I thought further about what was *really* happening.

There is a tension between those who espouse computer science theory and those who practice software as something of an engineering discipline. As I thought, I began to realize that here, in software metrics, is the lightning rod for that tension. The harsh question from the audience was the lightning bolt, the inevitable result of that tension.

Metrics vary in difficulty from those that are easy to obtain to those that are hard. But when looked at in the context of other computer science interest areas, even the hardest of the metrics is still easy to examine and evaluate. That is, it is much easier to try to validate a metric than to validate, for example, the quantitative value of Parnas's principles of information hiding. No one doubts the value of Parnas's work and the value of appropriate modularization, but no one really has any idea how much better software is when it has those characteristics than when it does not.

So here, in software metrics, people can not only choose up sides about the value of academic computer science theory, but they can also point with either pride or disdain to the measurement of that value from easily obtained results.

In a very important way, that's too bad. Because tangled in amongst the entrepreneurial hype and the theoretic advocacy, there is an important reality to software metrics. We may not have found the right ways to do it yet, but it is vital that we keep trying. If Halstead was wrong, what is right?

Can we learn anything about building software in the future based on the numeric artifacts gathered from dusty past efforts?

Surely, the answer will eventually be "Yes."

And when that happens, perhaps lightning will no longer strike at those who stand up and talk about software metrics.

Quality Measurement: Less Masquerading as More

Have you shopped for CASE tools lately? Have you looked at tools for measuring the quality of your software? If you have, you know that, with your purse strings open wide enough, you can buy all the quality measurement tools you might want.

The big question is, how many might you want? Or, putting it another way, are those quality measurement tools really worth buying?

As we pursue the answer to *that* innocent-looking question, we open the door to a whole lot of interesting side issues: "Are there different ways of measuring quality?" "If there are, which ones are best?" And "Do we really need a tool to measure quality?"

The quick answers to those side issue questions are "Yes," "We'll talk about it," and "Probably not." Let's look at what lies behind those quick answers.

Are there different ways of measuring quality?

Yes, there are several different ways of measuring quality. In fact there are essentially two quality measurement camps, one of which you've probably heard of, and one of which you may not have.

The best-known quality measurement camp relies on academic computer science theory to measure quality by the complexity of the software product. The advocates of complexity measures say that complex software is hard to understand, hard to modify, perhaps unreliable, and perhaps less efficient than it could be. That is, indeed, a pretty good summary of quality traits. At first glance, the use of complexity to measure quality seems very encouraging.

There is a problem with complexity measures, however. For one thing, different complexity measures are advocated by different theorists. Some say we should measure complexity by measuring operators and operands in a program; others say to count decision points; others count statement types, or executable statements, or connections between data items, or connections betyween logic points, or errors, or testedness, or . . . Name a measure, and someone probably uses it as a measure of complexity.

Now it turns out the diversity of measures, interestingly enough, isn't that much of a problem for complexity measures. That's because most of the measures, according to computer science researchers who have done comparative measurements, agree with each other. That is, given a piece of real software, most complexity measures give roughly the same answer. But, and this is a big BUT, you can get the same answer by counting lines of source code. And that, of course, is so easy to do that it's trivial!

The fundamental problem with the most-used complexity measures, then, is that there's an easy way to obtain their equivalent. And if that's so, then why bother to buy a tool to do it?

There's another fundamental problem with complexity measures. Remember that the underlying assumption is that complexity is a bad thing, and software that gets a high complexity rating is of low quality. But what if the problem being solved by the software is in fact very complex? Normally, we know that complex problems warrant complex solutions. So if a piece of software gets a high complexity rating, it could simply mean that the software engineers who built it had a particularly nasty problem to solve.

Now this latter problem can be overcome, of course. Software that gets a high complexity rating, whether by lines of code ratings or more complicated techniques, is simply a *candidate* for further analysis. Maybe the software is needlessly complex, in which case it should be simplified. But maybe the software engineer simply couldn't avoid building a complex product. Good analysis should be able to tell the difference.

Another community heard from

But complexity is not the only way, as it turns out, to measure software quality. Remember that complexity measures have been developed in the academic computer science theory community? Well, there's another community doing interesting work in quality measurement. It's a corner of the research world we hear a lot less about—the military-funded research world. But the work done in this community is more comprehensive and in many ways more interesting than the world we've just finished discussing.

In this latter community, the idea is to measure quality by a more complete set of traits than just complexity. Quality is, in fact, broken down into a set of constituent elements, and then each of those elements is measured. The elements should sound familiar to you; most people include in their definitions of software quality things like portability, reliability, efficiency, human engineering, understandability, testability, and modifiability. Those are the elements that this community uses to measure quality. (Actually, the Air Force studies involve 13 such elements).

The idea is that if we can measure each of these elements, and assign a relative importance to each one for a particular product, then we can measure the quality of that product by doing a summation:

Quality = SUM(quality element score*quality element importance)

And the problem then becomes, how well can we measure the elements?

The people exploring the answer to this question are funded by a U.S. Air Force base in upstate New York. There, for more than a decade, a driving interest in software quality has resulted in a series of studies conducted on their behalf by various industrial organizations. Early on, much of the work was done by researchers at General Electric. More recently, Boeing has been very active in the research.

What have they done? They have developed a worksheet approach to measuring each of the quality elements. For each quality element, a lengthy worksheet lists the information that must be recorded to obtain a measurement. Worksheet factors include things like the number of major functions, or the number of logic paths, or the number of overlays. The information-gathering process tends to be manual and slow. In verification exercises, users have reported spending 4 to 25 hours per metric worksheet.

Given all these approaches, which ones are best?

We've already discussed the value of the complexity metrics approach. Given all the ways of calculating complexity, the simple measure "lines of source code" seems to be as good as any. But how do these Air Force studies play against lines of code?

To be brief, there's a problem. Here again, there is good news and there is bad news. The good news is that evaluation contractors, people paid by the Air Force to evaluate the work done to date, find the results "sound" and "reasonable," and say that the findings "match the developers' intuition" about product quality. But the bad news is that they also find the measurement techniques "arbitrary" and lacking in a "real-world basis for the contentions of the measurement methodology." More telling than that, no practitioners anywhere appear to be using these quality measurement approaches. That could be, of course, because this community is little understood outside the military world. But more likely, it is because the cost of doing the measurement doesn't produce enough benefits to make it worthwhile.

Do we really need a tool to measure quality?

So what's the bottom line here? There are lots of quality measures. There are even two rather different communities working on two rather different approaches. But the fact of the matter is, none of them appear to have big payoff in the world of software reality.

If you need to measure the quality of your software, or the quality of the software you buy from others, there's probably no substitute at this point for doing some heavy-duty unautomated analysis using top-notch evaluators.

Sure, you can buy a tool to help out if you want to. But that tool won't tell you much more than the number you can get off the bottom of your compilation listing—the number of source lines in the program.

If you'd like to learn more about the Air Force quality measurement project, contact:
Roger B. Panara
Rome Air Development Center
Air Force Systems Command
Griffiss Air Force Base NY 13441

Can You MANAGE Quality
Into a Software Product?

Is software quality a management topic or a technical topic?

A lot of people see it as the former. If you read a book on software quality, or take a course on software quality, there is a tacit assumption that right after the word "quality" will be found the word "assurance." With that addition certainly quality becomes a management topic.

But I don't see that addition as necessary. I believe that the fundamental problem in software quality is technical, not managerial, and I would like to decouple the word "quality" from the word "assurance."

Now this technology-first approach requires an explanation. Let's take a look at the management and the technology of software quality.

No matter how carefully management plans for and provides for quality processes in software development, I believe that it is no more possible to *manage* quality into a software product than it is to *test* it in. It is well accepted that quality cannot be tested into software (because testing only looks at reliability, one facet of quality, and because testing comes too late in the life cycle to have a preventive effect on poor quality), but it is not at all commonly accepted that quality cannot be managed in. In fact, that is a radical viewpoint.

The reason I believe that you can't *manage* in quality is that quality is a deeply intimate software trait. As we explore what quality *really* is, we see that the injection of quality, and the detection of quality, occur far below the surface of software's facade. How can you put understandability and modifiability, two of quality's attributes, into a software product? How can you find out if they were put there? There are no easy answers to those questions, but the fact is that only a technical person can do the putting and the finding. Understandability and modifiability are so deeply technical that it is simply not assessable by the casual viewer. Management, for better or worse, is in this sense only a casual viewer of the software product. Management in general is not and should not be comfortable with the technical tasks necessary for either instilling or detecting understandability and modifiability.

And those are not the only two examples of technology's key role in quality. Software must be reliable, nearly always. Software must be portable, at least sometimes. Both are quality attributes. Who but a technical specialist can truly insure that software is reliable, or distinguish between portable and nonportable software? Most managers have either atrophied capabilities, or none at all, in these areas.

That is not to say, of course, that management has no role in building quality software. To the contrary, there is an essential role for management to play. Management must construct and maintain a climate in which quality is fostered and nurtured.

What do I mean by a quality climate? One where processes which facilitate quality are enabled and followed. One in which tools to assist in providing quality are procured and used. One in which people who think quality are hired and helped. One in which advocacy of product quality occurs right up there with advocacy of schedule and cost constraint conformance.

It is easier to say those things than to do them. We are passing through an era in which schedule and cost have been the dominant factors in evaluating software management and software products. There are some good reasons for that. Software's schedule and cost performance have often been abysmal. With rampant problems in that area, management has rightfully concentrated on trying to solve those problems.

But there is a danger here. As the pressure of meeting schedule and reducing cost intensifies, it is quality that inevitably suffers. How can we accelerate a late product? Cut back on whatever is happening when the problem is discovered, usually verification and testing. The result is reduced product quality.

The software manager of the twenty-first century must find a new equation for software. It must not simply be

software product = on schedule + within budget

It must instead be

software product = quality + on schedule + within budget

And achieving good results in that more complicated equation requires management commitment to quality as an end goal right up there with schedule and cost.

Fortunately, it is not hard for management to facilitate the construction of quality software. Most technical people fundamentally want to do a good, quality job. In fact, sometimes in the tradeoffs between quality and cost and schedule, technical people lean too heavily on the side of quality! (Steve Jobs, during a 1989 interview, said ". . .our jobs as senior managers are to help people get very clear on the goals . . . and then to get the hell out of their way.") Management usually will find very willing partners in the task of facilitating quality software.

So there it is. In the business of software quality, the technical considerations are much more complex and vital than the management ones. Quality assurance is important, but it is only one avenue to software quality.

Let me try a little exercise with you. I will now say the word "quality." See if you can avoid hastily adding the unwritten additive "assurance."

Quality.

There, that wasn't so hard, was it?

The Legend
of the
Bad Software Project

Once upon a time there was a software practitioner who got in BIG trouble. The trouble this practitioner got into was that his software was over budget, behind schedule, and unreliable.

What's so unusual about that, you may be thinking, if you've read the literature on the so-called software crisis.

Well, for this fellow it *was* unusual. And for a lot more than you'd think, I'd like to add. You see, this software practitoner had graduated from one of the best computer science schools in the land. He had several years of good solid programming experience after that. He'd even found a way to blend the best of what he'd learned in school with the best of the practice over those several years.

In other words, this software practitioner was all the things a good software practitioner should be. So what went wrong?

It all started back when the problem his program solved first surfaced. This was a hot problem, one with the potential for making a lot of money for the company. Management told him so. Marketing told him so. There seemed little doubt that this particular problem needed to be treated in a special way.

The first special way that it needed to be treated was that it had to be done by a particular date. Management said so. Marketing said so. Never mind that this particular practitioner didn't think it could be done by then. It had to be.

Being a cooperative fellow, the practitioner began work on the problem in spite of his concern. Management did listen to him and his concerns, though. While he developed the software, they tried a bunch of cost estimation modeling programs until they found one that gave the answer they wanted. "See," management pointed out to him with glee, "you can too develop this software in the time you have."

As time went on and the deadline approached, the practitioner grew more and more intense. At first he had taken care to develop the software to his own personal standards of quality, going over the requirements carefully, doing the design thoroughly, desk-checking each line of code with considerable thought.

But with the deadline at hand, the practitioner began to short-circuit good practice. Testing was done skimpily, with fingers crossed. Integration put together some modules that were tested with some that were not. Beta test got a product that wouldn't pass a normal internal test. But the deadline seemed sacred, and other things—seemingly, under the pressure, less important—were sacrificed.

In the end, the practitioner failed to meet the schedule, by about what his initial estimate said. Costs were higher than predicted, of course, because costs were predicted to the optimistic schedule. And reliability? It, too, had suffered, as the practitioner tried too many short cuts attempting to meet schedule. It was just like the software crisis people said—yet another software project behind schedule, over budget, and unreliable.

Once upon a time, in other words, a good software practitioner produced a bad software project. Deep down, the developer knew that he shouldn't have cut so many corners. But also deep down, the software developer knew that there had really only been one mistake in the development process.

That mistake was not in the way he built the software. Instead, it was in trying to meet a schedule that was wrong from the beginning.

When the software practitioner got his review from management, he noticed that he was graded down for poor performance on this bad project.

And he wondered. How many others suffered the same fate as he? How much of the software crisis was really due to poor or contrived estimation?

He is still wondering.

Would You Buy a Used Car from King Ludwig?

Full-page advertisements, in any computing publication, aren't cheap. Full-page color ads are even more expensive. In spades.

But this is the era of computer space wars. And the space that's being used is newspaper space, magazine space, and even television space. It's pretty hopeless to market a broad-appeal software product without buying some of that space. Or even a lot of that space.

You've probably seen examples of what I mean. Remember when Ring-a-ding Tel and Tel first brought out their new computer product line? They didn't just buy one-page ads. They didn't just buy one-page color ads. They bought several-page color ads. "Buy our product" was said in such a chunk of the periodical carrying the ad that no one could miss seeing it.

Or remember the software data base company that took their competitor on, head on? "R" product, they said with clever abbreviating, can beat theirs. And then they went on for several expensive pages to explain how.

With all that money pouring into advertising space, it makes sense that these companies would pour a comparable amount of money into advertising copy preparation. Most are. Traditional advertising agencies are developing a whole new skill set, learning how to hype software and hardware. It's a mass market out there in computing, now, folks, and we sell this stuff in the mass-market way. Like it or not.

All of that is prelude to the story I want to tell. This is a story about a software company that went the whole route. Full-page ads. Color added. Advertising agency. All the stuff we just talked about. They did it all right.

Except for one little thing.

Did you ever see a picture of Germany's Neuschwanstein castle? I'll bet you have, whether you recognize it or not. It's that medieval-looking, fortress-looking, high in the Bavarian Alps structure that adorns most travel brochures for Europe. Towers and turrets and tall trees around, in a mountain-top setting unbelievable in its grandeur.

There's a funny thing about that castle, though. It's kind of a fake. Oh, I don't mean it isn't there or anything. I mean it isn't medieval. And it was never a fortress. It was built by King Ludwig of Bavaria in the nineteenth century. Yes, the nineteenth century. That's not what you call medieval. And that's not when you needed a fortress. So Neuschwanstein, for all its grandeur, isn't quite what it appears to be.

There's another funny thing about King Ludwig's castle. And that's King Ludwig himself. History says, without much contradiction, that King Ludwig was something of an anachronism. He built a castle because he sort of wished it were the medieval era. He had a thing for French royalty, for instance, at a point in history where French royalty had just been guillotined out of existence. Some historians even say—and this one is not without contradiction—that old Ludwig was quite mad. It is true that he spent his kingdom into financial disarray, and he was spirited away before Neuschwanstein was fully finished.

Now let's tie a few loose ends together. Suppose you're the president of Security Software, and you have a brand new product that you want to market which protects data files by a combination of locks, passwords, and encryption. Super-strong protection is the name of the game. And in those expensive ads you know you're going to have to buy, you want something that gives an image of impregnable strength. How about good old Neuschwanstein Castle? Eye-arresting beauty, and the proper image besides. What a great advertising coup!

Well, in fact there is a Security Software—actually, a company with a different name, but in the same game—and that's exactly the route they chose. Great ad copy it made, too. Except for this one problem. The advertising agency apparently didn't know as much about Neuschwanstein as we do.

"The secret of King Ludwig's Castle," begins the ad copy. "High in the Bavarian Alps stands mighty Neuschwanstein Castle," it continues. And then it starts stepping onto shaky ground. "This magnificent medieval stronghold has taught us a valuable lesson in data security design. King

Ludwig's appreciation for detailed planning is what made Neuschwanstein the impregnable fortress that it was." And then the ad goes on to explain how Security Software offers the same kind of carefully-planned, impregnable defense against software intruders.

Well, I guess in a high-visibility, high-dollar world of software, we've invented a new set of ways to fail. Not just your software product can screw up. Your advertising gimmick can blow up in your face as well.

It's interesting to think a little further about the advertising game, though. If a software product is a mistake, it's a mistake, and it quietly fades from the marketplace. If an advertising product is a mistake, though, things may be different. Like the wind-dropped Tacoma Narrows bridge, the fame of your goof may well outlive the fame of your product. In a way, that's what I've proved by writing this article.

Still, though, picture this ultimate Neuschwanstein ad. There's the castle, and there's King Ludwig himself, standing in front of it, flags flying from all the castle's turrets. "Security Software" does the job, may be what the ad copy is saying. But the nagging, perhaps even subliminal response, is . . . "Would you buy a used car from this man?"

The Real Secrets of Consulting

by Nicholas Zvegintzov

Have you ever wondered about the real life of world-famous consultants? Is it all honors, $5,000 days, Concorde flights, keynote addresses, rich food, and groupies? In this tongue-in-cheek vision, Nicholas Zvegintzov, editor of "Software Maintenance News," piggybacks on the work of Jerry Weinberg (*The Secrets of Consulting—A Guide to Giving and Getting Advice Successfully,* Dorset House Publishing, 1985) to reveal the *real* secrets of consultants (or at least numbers 1 through 4!).

I fell asleep on Hermosa Beach, California, at 9 A.M. on a Sunday morning in January. When I awoke, three little surfers and a lifeguard in a beige jeep with a surfboard on the roof-rack were all staring at me. The boys were as stern as avenging Angelenos.

One said: "He wasn't surfing, skateboarding, jogging, or bicycling. He was snoring. It was *symphonic.*"

The second said: "I saw a 60's dope-head beach-bum once. Granddad knew him."

The third said: "If we turn him in, can we get a reward and be in a TV movie?"

The cop stroked his electric shark-stunner.

I said: "I'm a consultant from the east. I have jet-lag." I waved the red-covered book. "I fell asleep reading Weinberg's *The secrets of consulting*. *Datamation* asked me to review it. I promised to read it on the plane. James Martin called it 'Fun airplane reading for all consultants.' "

"I saw an airplane once from close," said one of the boys. "I rode all day on my skateboard and came to the edge of this great big old wide concrete field. It was *avionic*."

"Consultants come from airplanes," said another boy. "I learned that in sex education."

"Let me handle this, son," said the cop. "James Martin, isn't he the most influential DP guru of all time? I'd like to learn the secrets of consulting and be an influential DP guru! How could you fall asleep reading Weinberg's *The secrets of consulting?*"

"It's too mellow," I said.

The cop gave a low eerie growl and fingered the bear on his California shoulder patch. "How can something be too mellow?" he said.

I realized my mistake. "Well, not too mellow, but too good to be real. Weinberg says the secrets of consulting are being sensitive, humble, supportive, trustworthy, not demanding too much nor expecting too little."

The cop yawned. "I see what you mean. Those can't be the *real* secrets."

"They're not. The First Real Secret is that each consultant has exactly one message. James Martin says programmers cause backlog. Richard Nolan says that DP groups go through stages. T. Capers Jones says that secret data from IBM explains productivity. Harlan Mills says that math makes error-free systems. E.F. Codd says data are relational. Tom Gilb says you must design to measurable attributes. Weinberg says you make things work through technical leadership, not politics." I paused.

"Don't be modest, now," said the lifeguard. "What's *your* message?"

"Maintenance develops systems."

"I learned those Great Truths on the Western Civ video," said one of the boys proudly. "It was *eclectic*."

"Yes, but the Second Real Secret," I said "is that the message doesn't have to be true. In fact, some of the above messages (no names) are false."

"But how can a message be believed unless it is true?" said the cop.

"It doesn't have to be true, it only has to be attractive. Look around you." I pointed to the gorgeous skateboarders, joggers, and bicyclers on the strand.

The cop began to give that bear-growl again, so I hurried on to the Third Real Secret. "Consultants graze upon meadows of clients. When one meadow is exhausted, the consultant crosses the horizon to another. Boys, what's beyond California?"

"Nothing's beyond California," said one.

"*Northern* California," said another.

The third boy said: "My folks took me to Vegas once, but they made me stay in the kids dungeon at the hotel. It was *hermetic*."

"You got the right idea," I said. "Beyond California is Nevada, beyond Nevada is Utah, beyond Utah is Colorado, beyond Colorado is Nebraska. Weinberg lives in Nebraska."

"*Mesozoic*," said the boy who had been to Vegas.

"Wait a minute," said the Lifeguard. "What happens when a consultant finds that a meadow has been grazed already?"

"Ah, that's taken care of by the Fourth Real Secret. No two consultants eat the same food. If they keep moving, the grass is always green."

"How could that be?" said the lifeguard.

"Nature's magic," I said. "Have you ever heard of parthenogenesis?"

One of the boys said: "Is it like when Mom left and Dad's friend Uncle Bruce moved in and makes those desserts that catch on fire?"

"Close, but no goober. It's when everyone in the singles bar goes home alone—and figures they got lucky. Consultants are like that."

"But your Real Secrets are so cold" said the lifeguard. "Each consultant, for ever alone, doomed to draw nourishment from the eternal preaching of a single message? It is a vision of Hell. It is my avocation to guard life, but if these are the Real Secrets of Consulting, I should turn in my whistle and climb into my body-bag. It's as if the sun were hidden behind dark masses of vapor, water congealed into frozen flakes, the trees were bare, man's breath smoked, and a gob of phlegm would clink when it hit the iron earth."

"It's *arctic*," wailed the littlest surfer. Tears rolled down his rubber suit.

"Look what you've done," said the lifeguard. "Aren't you ashamed? How can I bring the sunshine back to these little guys?"

I stood up, shook the sand from the folds of my consultant's robe, and handed him Weinberg's *The Secrets of Consulting*. "Read them this," I said.

As I left the beach for breakfast at Jerry's On The Strand I saw three figures sitting at the lifeguard's feet, and I heard three voices cry: "*Epic! Mythic! Ecstatic!*"

Somehow, I knew which phrase from this review the publisher would use on the book cover.

A Look into
the Past of the Futurist

Prediction is a fascinating business.

Turn a major page on a calendar, and it's like turning the crank on a jack-in-the-box. Just as the melody really gets going, up pops a futurist, spouting uncontradictable wisdom about the era to come.

Now I haven't got anything against futurists. For one thing, looking into the future is a necessity. All of us want clues about what's to come, in order to know better what to do with what's already happened. For another thing, futurists liven up the place. If we all spent our time waddling around in the present, where would we get grist for our fantasies? All of us, in fact, are closet futurists. It's just that some of us aren't as good at it as others.

Which brings me to the point of this essay. There's a sadistic side of me that says "in this time of the decade of the 1990s, let's check out the accuracy of the futurists of the past." Are futurists, in fact, worth listening to? It's an honest, useful question to ask. Let's do it.

Tip-toe with me, if you will, into the library stacks of the past. Shh! Let's not tell our surrounding futurists what we're up to. Quietly, quietly, let's move swiftly over to the dusty computing periodicals of yesteryear.

Here, among pages ripe with pony-tailed young sex symbols selling computing products to crew-cut executives, are the futurists of the past. Now, let's listen. What are they saying?

Here's one now. It's January 1970, and one futurist is answering the architectural question of the 1970s. "The third-generation infant has toddled, walked, and now runs . . . Can another generation be far behind?" The answer, implicit in all that follows, is a resounding "No" [AMDA70].

Well, here we are many years later. The third-generation infant is still running, even though it looks a little different, what with all its facelifts. But basically, it's still the same child now grown older.

"But," you whisper quietly so as not to disturb our library stack neighbors or alert any listening futurists, "maybe that was just one futurist's view. Surely others knew that the calamity and wonder of generational change was nearly wound down?"

Ah-ha, here's another. It's still January 1970, and another futurist is saying "Let's predict the next generation will be along soon, that it will be incompatible, that the users will snap it up, that the errors of 1965 will be repeated and magnified, and that you read it here first" [DORN70]. No matter that there's a bit of tongue firmly in cheek here, things are getting worse, not better. Now the futurists are fighting to be first in line to be wrong! At least on major issues like new computing generations, the futurists were as good as out to lunch.

"Well, then, what about the microcomputer and distributed processing revolution as seen from the past?" you ask in hushed tones. "Surely the futurists saw that one coming." A good question. Let's check it out.

Here, in this library-stale-smelling periodical, is one futurist's answer. "All things considered, there would seem to be a developing tendency toward centralization for the large corporate user . . ." [AMDA70]. A little evasive, you say, what with all that "seems to be" and "larger coprorate user"? Well, what about this one: ". . . when it comes to general-purpose computing, the economies of scale are swinging increasingly in the direction of large machines" [SOLO66].

That one's fairly clear. These futurists have come down firmly on the wrong side of the micro and distributed processing fence.

Moving right along the stacks, let's take a look at software issues. It's 1970 still, and we're just beginning to recover from third-generation computers, and software "unbundling." Remember unbundling? In the early days of computing, all software came "free" with the hardware. (Free is in quotes because it was often true that the more expensive hardware just happened to have more software with it than cheaper hardware). Then, late in the 1960s, some of the hardware companies came to the farsighted conclusion that software costs too much to give it away, and then began charging for it separately, unbundling the cost out of the total hardware price. It was about this time that software entrepreneurs began salivating

heavily, fantasizing the potential profits right around the unbundled corner. In the midst of this anticipation, our futurists of the 1970s predicted
"the practice of separation between hardware and software sales may soon
see as many as 1,000 companies, each offering scores of software products
for sale" [BROM70].

Alas, like the other predictions of this essay, that futurist saw all too
clearly through a clouded crystal ball. The hardware companies, who could
read futurist predictions as well as the next computing person, set their
software prices carefully—just high enough to make money, but just low
enough to discourage predator companies—and the software entrepreneurial boom bombed. Not toally, of course. There are successful software
houses today, most of course spawned by the micro revolution and not
unbundling. But even yet, there are not hundreds of companies, each
offering scores of products.

Then let's try over here . . . see? It's a veritable treasure trove of past
futurism. It's a series of 1970s era interviews with "decision makers." Each
of the interviewees seems to be grinding his or her own axe, making a
prediction that matches what he or she wishes would happen. Now this is
a whole new kind of futurist, the kind who believes that predicting can
make it so. What did these attempts at self-fulfilling prophecy predict? Try
these on for size:

- On small computers . . . "Small businesses are not going to have
  small computers. It's not a practical way to go. Small companies are
  going to use a piece of a large computer" [BENN70].
- On the people problem . . . "As the industry matures and the pool of
  competent, experienced people expands . . . employers will have
  more candidates to choose from. . ." [PARR70].
- On programming languages . . . "I believe that a major change to
  come on the part of users will be a shift away from both COBOL and
  PL/I . . . The computer world keeps talking about COBOL as if they
  knew what they were talking about. But in the final analysis, it just
  won't work . . . COBOL is hopeless" [HARR70].
- On service bureaus . . . "Service bureaus are in for some major
  changes . . . The most major change will be a potential abandonment
  of dedicated in-house facilities by many companies" [YOUN70].

Talk about out to lunch! These futurists missed the boat (or at least the
dinner cruise) as well on such items as the microcomputer revolution, the
sometimes-troubling programmer shortage, the ubiquitousness of COBOL
(it's STILL number one on the programming hit parade), and the role of the
in-house computer. That's a pretty good grand slam of failed futurism!

Perhaps there is something unfair about this analysis? Well, of course there is. For one thing, the 1970 decade change was a peculiar era. Just as the field hit its growth stride (one leading computing trade journal went from once a month publication to twice a month in 1970, because their issues had gotten so thick that the binding could barely contain them), a major recession hit (and that same publication cut back to once a month tiny issues in early 1972). Even the people who published predictions had guessed wrong!

Then again, perhaps it's also unfair to focus on predictions made in the popular trade journals. Have the serious, scientific publications had something more accurate to say?

Over here, on this other set of library shelves, are some prestigious journals. Let's pull a couple of issues down and see what we find there.

For openers, there just aren't any blatant predictions here. Look at this end-of-the-decade 1960 issue. There's stuff on sorting, and character sets, but nothing on what the sorts or sets of the future might look like.

But then, in the serious journals *every* article is an implicit prediction. Have you heard computer scientists say that today's research is tomorrow's practice? Tomorrow, of course, is defined as a variable number of years, but still most people would define their tomorrow as "+10." So let's look again at these serious articles, and take a reading of those predictions.

For balance, let's look at the 1970s. If the popular journals were looking forward to fourth-generation hardware, centralized computers, and software package proliferation, what were the serious journals saying?

Here's an article on natural language translation. Oh, good, it won't be long before words, phrases and thoughts will be automatically translatable from Russian (say) into English. Except, there's an oops in the story. Oops— idioms and slang and multiple meaning words proved, over the years, to make all but the simplest word-for-word translation infeasible. Attempts to translate "Time flies like an arrow" stumbled over the noun/verb ambiguities of "time" and "flies," and as a result natural language translation flew like a heavily burdened, clipped-wing fly, and finally plummeted into the ground, to arise later only as assistants to human translators.

Here's another 1970s era computer science article, this time on Management Information Systems. Ah, the MIStique of the beginnings of the MIS era. What a shame it turned out to be, in many respects, a MIStake. We didn't know as much as we thought we knew, we can now see, about the information needs and methodologies of running an organization. The promise of the 1970s dissolved into the partially successful groping of the 1980s. Large-scale integrated MIS became a target that hardly anyone hit successfully.

Were the predictions of the serious scientists of the 1960s any better? Let's move down the stacks a decade, a few inches of printed matter, and take a look at some older computer science articles. Ah, here's one on theorem proving. We'll be using computers to evaluate and derive proofs for tough mathematical or philosophical questions in no time at all—that's the promise of the article. It was a promise to be left unfulfilled. Like the natural language translation era which followed, it foundered on the grubby details of the problem area.

So, if the popular journals aren't very reliable at predicting the future, and neither are the serious journals, then what's a computer person who cares about the future to do?

One obnoxious answer is to go ahead and read all the predictions, add a healthy measure of doubt, and file them away on a shelf to be looked at later, much as we just finished doing. But in the meantime, use them as the clouded crystal ball predictions that they are, educated guesses by educated people into a future which doesn't always behave in an educated fashion.

But there's another answer. It's the cowardly approach to predicting the future. What follows is a set of predictions made purely for the sake of boosting the predictor's average. They may not create a lot of fantasies, but they are backed by the knowledge of the solid, dull past.

So here they are. The frustrated, failed futurist takes a nonrisk, nonmyopic look into the highly visible future:

1. People will continue to make predictions about next-generation computers. Technical journals will continue to carry increasingly more accurate foresight on hardware-to-come. And, someday, those predictions will come true.

2. Computer hardware builders will continue to be congratulated on the breathtaking drop in the price of their products. People will continue to predict that *hardware* will soon be given away free with *software*, a rebundling years after unbundling.

3. Hardware improvements for the software builder will be nearly nonexistent. There will be no dramatic improvements in instruction sets or register conventions. The "Ada machines" and "Modula machines" of the decade ahead will be the same sales-puffed paper tigers as the "Fortran machines" and "COBOL machines" of 20 years ago.

4. People will continue to predict that automated generation of software by powerful utility programs is just around the corner. They will continue to be wrong, just as were their very bright colleagues of ten years ago, and twenty years ago.

5. Some academicians will continue to base both theory and practice on the belief that programs may be proven correct someday. Some industry specialists will ignore proof of correctness on the grounds that it is too hard, too costly, and too dubious. Time will prove the correctness of the industry approach.

6. Managers of software projects will insist on more and more English-readable documentation describing their programs. Software specialists will grit their teeth and produce that documentation, knowing that no one but them will ever know if it really matches the code.

7. Lecturers will get very rich presenting seminars on Ada. Theoreticians will both laud and ridicule that complex language. Pragmatisms will move fearfully toward the major new learning experience. Fortran and COBOL will, once again, survive.

8. The adjective "structured" will continue to be applied to every meaningful noun in the computing milieu. It will continue to mean whatever the author of the moment says it means. Lecturers will not get as rich presenting seminars on structured methodology as they did ten years ago.

9. Some of these "safe" predictions, like many of the more risky and interesting ones, will be wrong. But hardly anyone will be nasty enough to save this essay for the period of time necessary to show which are which!

Oh, and one last prediction, one with which no one will disagree:

10. Next year at the beginning of the year, the futurists will pop out of their jack-in-the-boxes again with a whole new set of predictions. And we will read them just as avidly as we did this year's!

REFERENCES

AMDA70   Lowell D. Amdahl, "Architectural Questions of the Seventies," *Datamation*, January 1970.

BENN70   William Bennett, "Decision Makers," *Computer Decisions*, January 1970.

BROM70   Howard Bromberg, "Revolution 1970," *Datamation*, January 1970.

DORN70   Philip A. Dorn, "The Onslaught of the Next Generation," Datamation, January 1970.

HARR70   Peter Harris, "Decision Makers," *Computer Decisions*, March 1970.

PARR70   Myron E. Parr, "Decision Makers," *Computer Decisions*, March 1970.

SOLO66   Martin B. Solomon, Jr., "Are Small Free-Standing Computers *Really* Here to Stay?" *Datamation*, July 1966.

YOUN70   Chester Young, "Decision Makers," *Computer Decisions*, March 1970.

User Support: There's More Here than Meets the Eye

The phone rings. Again. It's another customer with another question about The Product. Here you are, in charge of User Support for The Product, and the best you can hope for as you grab the phone is that the customer has read the user manual. But your best guess is that they haven't!

You're part of a big industry, you know. Ashton-Tate has 42 service representatives and gets 1,100 calls/day. Microsoft tops that with 50 reps and 1,800 calls/day. And WordPerfect has 31 phone lines to handle 2,500–3,500 calls/day. Little did your company know, when they conceived of The Product and thought of marketing it for the first time, how big a deal the Big Deal of user support really was. There's a lot more to software maintenance than just software maintenance, they had learned.

Since you became head of User Support for The Project, you've done a little research into the subject. You know that calls cost Living Videotext about $30–$50 per hour to service. You know that, in spite of such impressive statistics, many calls at many companies go unanswered. And you learned what you didn't want to learn—that 70 percent of all callers haven't read the manual!

You even know where this User Support function fits into the corporate organization chart, and it's way up there. Lotus has a Vice President of Information Services and another of Publishing. Ashton-Tate has a Vice-President of Documentation and Communication, and another for Systems Services and Information. This User Support stuff is big money and a big deal.

In fact, you've checked into the options for User Support. You know that, besides telephone consultation and user manuals, there are several other choices:

1. HELP facilities. Software products contain their own user support mechanisms. Many companies, especially Lotus and Microsoft, are big on that.
2. Bulletin board forum. On the bulletin board, users can post questions and ideas and inquiries, and other users can respond. In fact, at companies like Borland and Software Publishing and others, the company reads the board every X hours, say X = 36, and answers the questions that remain unanswered.
3. Dealer reliance. Some companies, like Software Publishing, have maneuvered user support into a dealer function. Callers to those companies are simply referred to the dealer for help.
4. User groups. The users meet periodically and discuss their problems and solutions. This one is politically risky, some companies say. An empowered user may ask more of a company than it is willing to give.
5. Advisory committees. People knowledgeable in your customer industry meet regularly and give you advice on new directions for your product.
6. Newsletters. You can broadcast information about your product on a regular basis through a newsletter.
7. User surveys. You can poll your users and pass the results on inside your company and to the users as well.
8. Directories. You can simply let your users know who they are and where to find each other.

And in fact, you've even learned about some interesting information sources if you and your consultants want to learn more in depth about the topic. The Corporate Learning Institute at Vanderbilt University offers a course in "Consultation Skills," one week in length, in which there is hands-on and role-playing training in user support. The Institute for International Research advertises in *Software Maintenance News* a three-day course on "Software Support" which focuses on software-specific consulting. The notion of the Information Center, which among other things is a user-support facility for in-house users, has been often discussed in the literature, and there is a periodical published on the subject. And there are even companies in the social services field that publish books and hold workshops on topics like "Staying on Track Under Pressure" and "Dealing Effectively With Difficult People." (You found that latter one especially valuable!)

In other words, from the moment you were put in charge of User Suport, you treated it like any other problem to be solved. You found out what the body of knowledge was, and you absorbed as much of that body of knowledge as you could. What surprised you, after a rough start trying to find anything at all, was how much material there was out there.

But none of that matters right now. The phone has been ringing all through this reverie. You pick it up, and sure enough, there is a customer at the other end with a plaintive cry.

"How do I get 'Function A' to work on The Product," they say, a tiny note of panic in their voice.

"That's described on page six of the user manual," you respond. "Have you read that yet?" you say, trying not to scold, trying to hide the fact that only a dolt wouldn't have read to page six.

"Well, now, I didn't," says the user. "But I need to use that function right away." You can almost hear tears in the user's voice.

You smile the smile of the knowing. You put on a verbal mask of patience. "Well, here's how it works," you begin.

At least you know the customer will be paying your company $45 an hour for your help.

From the Laboratories

Structured Research?
(A Partly Tongue-in-Cheek Look)

There is a problem hardly anyone wants to talk about, but I think it's time to bring it out into the open. It's what I'd like to call the "software research crisis."

The software research crisis? What *is* this crisis? I hear you saying.

It's the tendency of research to be over budget, behind schedule, and unreliable. And it's a real crisis. When did *you* last hear of a research project that worked to a tightly controlled budget, came through on a predictable schedule, and was reliable enough to be put to immediate productive use?

I am not here just to bemoan this crisis. I have positive suggestions as to what we should do about it.

First of all, I think it is time we structure our research. In fact, I would like to propose a structured revolution for research.

What do I mean by structured research? First, we need a disciplined, rigorous, orderly, straightforward process for doing research. None of those random opportunistic "goto's." None of that slovenly, uncontrolled, freedom-loving serendipitous stuff out of the past. We will have a research life cycle, carefully controlled milestones for monitoring research accomplishments, and a set of research documents to be produced along the way so that management can get visibility into research progress.

And research metrics. We need ways of measuring both the productivity and the success of research projects. (Perhaps we could measure person-hours per Source Line Of published research Paper (SLOP)). In order to compare future research under this new paradigm with the undisciplined research of the past, we'd better begin collecting these metric data now. Contemporary research metrics data collection is perhaps the most urgent need of the research crisis.

Ah, and then we need to define research process. Perhaps we could even define a research process model, and invent a process language in which we could define the activities of research and monitor a specific project against that model.

What would be in the process model? First of all we would have all the elements of the research life cycle. We would define the requirements for the research in a formal, rigorous, mathematical language so that we could clearly convey them to our funding sources. In fact, with a rigorous enough language, perhaps we could look forward in the future to the automatic generation of research findings from these rigorous requirements languages.

And then we would have research design. Perhaps we could have a research design methodology, the Gane-Sarson or the Yourdon of research, a set of orderly steps and processes for doing design. And when we finished the design, we could represent that design in a collection of structured languages: idea flow diagrams (IFDs), in which the flow of ideas and the processes that manipulate them could be shown; research structure charts (RSCs), in which a hierarchic view of the research functions could be represented; and research design languages (RDLs), in which we could represent in a rigorous way the many miniscule details of the design. In fact, even without automatic generation of research from requirements specifications, we could probably, with the help of rigorous and thorough design representations, use technicians to finish the research once thorough designs were written.

And then research implementation. With all the formalization of the preceding processes, research implementation should be straightforward. We will have research design folders (RDFs), a sort of repository in which we put everything pertaining to the research implementation for the future use of whomever looks at RDFs, and we will hold research structured walkthroughs (RSWs), in which research peers will examine and critique research implementation findings. And we will get ready for the research testing process.

There are two possible approaches to structured research testing. The traditional approach, of course, is via the use of sample inputs, either structured or random (statistical), where test cases are run against the implemented research in order to seek flaws in its implementation. Or there is formal verification of the research, in which mathematical proof processes are used on the research findings to both seek errors and to prove the correctness of the results. Either way, these testing processes will be performed to structured test plans and be reported in structured test reports.

And maintenance? Well, of course, there is no maintenance problem in research (or if there is, it is the same as the research development process) and so we will not define a separate research maintenance process. (Note that here alone we have saved 40 to 80 percent of the research budget).

Now, with this rigorous approach to research, we can finally get control of these researchers. We can estimate the time it will take to do research from estimates of the lines of published papers that will result. And with appropriate estimates based on these structured and rigorous approaches, we can then more tightly control and monitor research, eventually solving the research crisis.

There is one more facet of contemporary research approaches to be dealt with. Current research is heavily ego based, with both institutional and self-belief intimately tied to the work and its publication. Research must be freed from its ego dependence. To do this, regular reviews will be held, matching the phases of the research life cycle, to monitor progress in front of both managers/customers and research peers. Then there will be aperiodic audits performed, to check troubled research projects for inherent flaws, and of course to enforce the structuring process on those projects that are trying to avoid its use. The result will be a team-based, egoless approach to research.

And there it is. With a well-defined research process program, appropriate discipline applied to researchers, a research life cycle with milestones by which we can measure research progress, reviews and audits for getting visibility into the process, and metrics to evaluate how well we did when the research ends, we can begin to control this elusive area.

Researchers of the world, rejoice! The structured revolution is at hand, the enforced discipline of rigorous and formal methods is coming, and the research crisis will soon be solved!

(This research was funded by the International Theological Society for Research and Other uncontrolled Things (ITSROT), and the author wishes to thank them for making this work possible. In particular, it is important that the sponsors did not insist that *this* research be subject to the proposals contained herein. These ideas, of course, are for *other* researchers and for software engineers, not for elite people such as myself).

The (Solved, Unsolved) Problem of Literature Searches

I hate to take something that seems simple and make it complicated. But sometimes, I guess, it has to be done.

The simple thing I want to talk about here is information gathering. How do you go about getting more information than you currently have on a particular topic? Let's say you're researching CASE tools, and you know a lot has been written on them in the last five years, and you'd like to read some of it.

Fundamentally that *is* a simple problem. Presuming you have access to a reasonably modern library system, you simply invoke a literature search system or person to look for references to CASE tools in the literature over the last five years. Modern library technology solves that problem rather well. You will get back a list of abstracts of relevant articles, and then you can look at the abstracts to select those papers you really want to read. Easy as can be.

Except that there is a problem. The library literature search processes appear to leave out two major sources of information. One is government reports. The other is vendor materials. The result of that problem is that when you do a literature search you only come up with about half the information you ought to have on any given topic.

If that's true, how come nobody has pointed this out before? After all, the age of our literature search system usage is now measured in decades. Surely someone would've noticed such a significant omission?

This is a case of mass myopia. If everyone is doing literature searches the same way, then who will notice that anything is missing? It's only if someone discovers unreported sources that it becomes apparent that there's a problem.

Let me give you a couple of examples.

If you look at the literature of software metrics, you will find a great deal of material. Wonderful and exciting books. Good and recent research studies. Innovative new ideas. But what you will *not* find is any reference to the quality metric work at Rome Air Development Center. For over a decade, the folks there have been funding research into measuring software quality. They've produced a lot of reports, many of them as good as anything published in the more traditional computer science literature. But I don't know of any work in any leading journal that references this material. And it's because these government reports, and many others like them, simply don't appear in the periodic literature and therefore in the standard literature search.

Here's another example. Several years ago, I wrote a survey article on software toolsets, producing a matrix of software tools and their functional capabilities. At the time, I had the nagging feeling that something important was being left out. Slowly it dawned on me. I may have summarized the functional capabilities of toolsets mentioned in the literature, but I had left out the most commonly used toolsets of all—those distributed by the computer hardware vendors. Information from those sources simply hadn't shown up in any of the literature searches I'd run.

In other words, researchers of any stripe who are relying on contemporary literature searches for complete access to relevant information are simply not getting what they think they are getting.

There's the problem. Gathering information is much more complex than the too-simple solutions we have available to us now.

What are some solutions? Well, for one thing researchers should contact the National Technical Information Service (NTIS) to find out about relevant government reports. But even that isn't enough. It appears to be true that some government documents important to our field don't make it into their listings.

For another thing, researchers should know about relevant products and contact product vendors. True, with vendor information you have to sift through a lot of marketing hoopla to learn what you really need to learn, but it's always in there if you dig hard enough. The hard part is not sifting through what you get, but knowing whether you've made enough contacts to cover the topic in question.

What else can we do? I don't like my answer. Keep your ears open for who's doing relevant work, and contact them. Scan listings of government documents. Keep in touch with relevant vendors. But all of a sudden these are difficult answers to a question we thought was simple. Making all these separate contacts is adding up to a lot of hard work.

I don't have any easy answers. If you do, I'd love to hear from you. How do YOU make sure your information investigations are complete?

A Tiny Controversy:
Some Pros and Cons on
(of all things!)
References

Should references to the literature be used in articles for professional journals? That doesn't seem like a very controversial issue, now, does it?

To me, though, it is. Let me explain why by taking a look at quotations from two book reviews in the March 1989 issue of *IEEE's Computer*.

In one, the reviewer discusses "a statement that. . .needs to be backed up with a reference to a book or article. . ." In the other, the reviewer concludes that the author "attempts to envelop the discussion in an academic aura, complete with references to other publications. . ." In these two reviews, we see a "damned if you do, damned if you don't" problem.

When do you reference and when do you not? I have an unusual belief in that regard. For openers, if you write for the professional/societal press, you use lots of references; if you write for the popular press, you don't. There's not a right or wrong way here, there are just societal norms.

But my unusual belief is that, although I strongly believe in the use of references when references are in order, especially to substantiate viewpoints and conclusions, I also believe that we have gone too far in their advocacy.

Take the first reviewer just quoted. The author has stated a conclusion, and the reviewer is saying that it should be substantiated. But in this case, the author of the book is a prime source of information, and may well be expressing a view that no one has expressed before. Because of that, there probably are no references. How, then, could the author be expected to come up with any? And as an alternative, should the author not have stated the conclusion if it couldn't be substantiated?

Let me put my belief succinctly. The use of references when there are any is important. But the expectation of references for material that is new thinking is unfair, and, worse yet, will tend to suppress seminal ideas.

And in this young field of ours, we need all the seminal ideas we can get.

How About Next Year?
A Look at a Study
of Technology Maturation

Did you ever wonder about how long it takes for new ideas in software to work their way into practice?

Well, a few years ago so did two well-known computer scientists, Sam Redwine and Bill Riddle, who at the time were working for the government's Institute for Defense Analysis and a private company called Software Design and Analysis, respectively.

Redwine and Riddle decided to satisfy their curiosity in a fairly rigorous manner. So they picked a dozen or so technologies, and they defined the steps a technology has to go through in order to mature. Then they researched the formal and informal literature just to see when each of those technologies reached each of those steps.

To make sure they got each technology off on an equal footing, they were careful to count the steps clear back to the beginning of the concept. So they defined those steps as:

0. emergence of the key idea
1. definition of a solution approach via a seminal paper or a demonstration system

2. usable capabilities available
3. shift to usage outside of development group
4. substantial evidence of value and applicability

In other words, the time span Redwine and Riddle were examining had to cover the first twinkling of an idea clear out to heavy usage in practice.

What kind of technologies did they pick? A mix of high-level and not so high-level ideas, like structured programming, software engineering, and Unix. There were 14 such technologies in all. Many of the technologies had not yet progressed through all five (0–4) steps. For example, knowledge-based AI approaches, Redwine and Riddle decided, have only reached step 2; and the use of software cost-estimation models has reached only step 3.

Now, with all of that as introduction, what's the bottom line? To tell the truth, it's discouraging. Those technologies which ever make it to step 4 tend to take 15 to 20 years to do it. That means that the technologies which are just making it into practice today were first conceived back in the early 1970s. And ideas which someone is conceiving today won't make it into practice until after the turn of the century.

Redwine and Riddle weren't content with this bottom line, however. Once they learned how long it had taken, they began thinking about and analyzing ways of improving the process. They came up with the following set of potential accelerators:

- *Conceptual Integrity.* If the idea is well thought through at the outset, it will avoid the controversy which otherwise slows the development of new ideas.
- *Clear Recognition of Need.* The need attacked by the idea must be well understood and clearly articulated.
- *Tuneability.* The idea must be easily bent to match other needs related to the original one.
- *Prior Positive Experience.* Reports of positive experiences with related technology will help.
- *Management Commitment.* Management responsible for the idea must support its development.
- *Training.* User training must be provided when the time comes.

Even with such advantages working for an idea, the evolution into practice will still simply be on the low side of that 15 to 20 year span. Major acceleration beyond that would happen only in extremely unusual circumstances.

There is confirmation of these findings elsewhere, by the way. These same kind of numbers have been obtained for other disciplines.

So if you have this hot new idea—I mean, a really fundamentally new idea—and you're planning on capitalizing on it in a big way sometime next year, the message here is clear. Don't hold your breath. As Redwine and Riddle put it, "technology maturation generally takes much longer than popularly thought." (If you want to read the whole original paper, it's in the *Proceedings of the 8th International Conference on Software Engineering*, held in London August 28–30, 1985. The sponsor and publisher is IEEE).

Software Technology Transfer:
A Multi-Flawed Process
(The Road to
Productivity is
Full of Potholes)

Anyone active in the software field is familiar with its enormous projected growth and the resultant predicted shortage of capable personnel.

With that knowledge, anyone active in the software field is also aware of the importance of technology transfer. A shortage of skilled personnel must be made up for by upgrading the skills, strengthening the support tools, and increasing the productivity of those who *are* in the field.

From here on the subject of technology transfer, as I see it, is a battleground of major proportions, one where progress is and will continue to be difficult or impossible.

Why do I feel that way? Why do I see software technology as a battleground rather than the cooperative search for progress it ought to be?

In order to answer that question, let me present an idealized view of technology transfer:

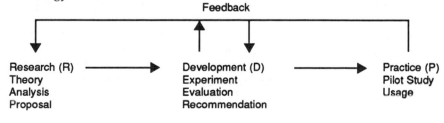

Feedback

Research (R)   ⟶   Development (D)   ⟶   Practice (P)
Theory   Experiment   Pilot Study
Analysis   Evaluation   Usage
Proposal   Recommendation

In this idealized picture, there are three agents; the researcher, designated "R"; the developer, designated "D"; and the practitioner, designated "P". The researcher develops theory and analyzes the results and proposes new concepts. The developer experiments with those concepts in an environment between that of the researcher and the practitioner and evaluates the experimental results and recommends technologies worthy of transition. The practitioner further explores the validity of the technologies using practice-oriented pilot studies, and makes use of those technologies that have passed all the hurdles.

So far in this discussion, information is flowing from left to right across the diagram. That information loop must be completed. The researcher must find out from the practitioner and from the developer which theories made it into practice, which did not, and why not. Furthermore, the researcher must gather ideas for new useful explorations and theories from the practitioner.

As I mentioned, this is an idealized picture of technology transfer. In what ways is the ideal not met in contemporary technology transfer? My answer is that very little of this idealized picture is working in practice.

Regarding the individual agents, I see this:

1. *Research.* The research component of the technology transfer process is strong. Theory development is healthy, analysis is intelligent, and proposed concepts are numerous. The research world has some tendency to follow fads, so that too much energy is spent in too few interest areas. But in general research is, as a stand-alone element, doing its part of the job.

2. *Development.* Here is the first major flaw in the technology transfer process. In our technical society, there are very few people interested in or doing the "D" of "R&D." As a result, this vital bridge between research and practice is unusable, and theory essentially cannot make it into usage. (It is interesting to note that in Japanese society there is considerably less emphasis on "R," and considerably more on "D," than in our own. I would assert that this accounts for the dramatic progress of the Japanese technically in this century).

3. *Practice.* The practice component of the technology transfer process is also strong. This is a controversial viewpoint. There is a litany that "software is always behind schedule, over budget, and unreliable" which has seized the limelight in discussions of the state of the practice. But the fact of the matter is, practitioners have solved extraordinarily difficult problems using a technology that most acknowledge is the most complicated ever undertaken by humanity, and that is the state of the practice only 30-odd years after its inception! True, practi-

tioners avoid risk and thus are reluctant to use new technologies, but compelling new technologies make it past this barrier regularly.

Regarding the communication links in the diagram, with the near absence of the "D" function, the left-to-right communication line is hopelessly broken. But the problem gets worse. The feedback (right-to-left) line at the top of the chart is nearly nonexistent as well. For a variety of reasons, very little information filters back from "P" people to "R" people. One reason is that "P" people are exasperated with the practical naivete of "R" people and don't find it useful to talk to them. "R" people, on the other hand, find "P" people backward and thus not interesting to talk to. (The choice of the words "useful" and "interesting" here was deliberate. The practitioner builds an ethic around working with that which is useful. The researcher builds an ethic around working with that which is interesting. Where ethics clash, it is not unusual to find communication breaks down).

As a result, although the absence of the "D" person is an obvious and serious failure in the technology transfer process, the absence of P → R communication is even more deadly. Attempts to do technology transfer in spite of these flaws have resulted in the battleground that I mentioned earlier.

I would assert that, as long as the "D" component is missing from the diagram, software technology transfer will largely fail. But even if the "D" problem were solved, the P → R communication gap must be substantially repaired or technology transfer will still fail. (It is worth noting that the presence of a "D" person in the loop may help bridge this P → R problem).

What can be done about this dilemma? The solutions at the superficial level are obvious. We must generate "D" people. We must foster P → R communication, in part by diminishing ethical barriers.

Those solutions are easy to advocate but hard to bring about. By what process will we get our society interested in producing "D" people? By what process do we foster communication between two camps presently armed and on a battleground? Those are societal problems as much as they are technical problems, and they are very hard ones.

I have found my own personal solution to this dilemma. After nearly 30 years in industry (first as a "P" person, then increasingly as a "D" person) I made the move several years ago to academia. Education and training are obviously at the heart of whatever solutions are eventually undertaken, and I am proud to have taught in the Master of Software Engineering (MSE) program at Seattle University.

The nominal purpose of the MSE program is to take functioning "P" people and make them better at what they do. But my personal purpose in being there was to help those "P" people who wanted to become "D" people to do so. Within the education provided at Seattle University is the nucleus of a "D" education. I fervently believe in the potential for what may be done there.

It is not enough to transition "P" people into "D" people, however. Some "R" people are going to have to make that transition as well. I would assert that our country is overloaded with people wanting to do "R"; my hope is that several people in the computer science academic world will see the value of what I am talking about here, and encourage and assist those students who are "R" bound but interested in and good at "D."

If technology transfer is to work, in other words, several things must happen:

1. Development people must be created to bridge the gap between theory and practice. The source for those people must be *both* the research world and the practitioner world.

2. Research people must listen to practitioners. Just because something is theoretically sound does not mean it will work in practice. The experience that practitioners bring to a problem has value.

3. Practitioners must listen to development people. Just because something is theoretically sound does not mean that it will *fail* to work in practice! The knowledge that R&D brings to a problem has value.

It is only with *all* the participants playing together that technology transfer and its attendant productivity gains can have any hope of working.

A Mythology of
Technology Transfer

There was a workshop on Software Technology Transfer at Santa Fe not too long ago. People at the conference struggled with the issue, "How can we take the best of computing research and get it used in practice?"

That, of course, is one of the key issues of software productivity. But it's a complicated issue. First of all, what is the "best" of computing research? How do we screen out the "worst" of computing research and not waste our time trying to transfer that? How do we motivate the practitioner to try something new, given such real problems as risk, cost, and schedule pressure?

One of the presenters at the workshop, Patrick O'Brien of Digital Equipment Corp., showed another dimension of the complexity of the problem. He discussed what he called "A Mythology of Technology Transfer," and he presented seven myths for consideration. Here they are (the myths are O'Brien's, the wording of the rationales is mostly my own):

- *Myth 1.* The corporate research group has sole responsibility for innovation.

    Wrong! If the application practitioner isn't constantly looking for new and better ways of taking care of business, vital new ideas will be missed. Innovation must not be delegated.

- *Myth 2.* Since development and research groups stand to gain so much from collaboration, they will gladly cooperate and interact to transfer technology.

  Wrong again! If it's not politics, it's NIH ("not invented here.") Some people won't cooperate unless you lock them in a room and don't let them out until they do.

- *Myth 3.* The great innovations (that make a real impact on the company) result from significant new technological breakthroughs.

  Maybe yes, maybe no. But marketing may drag in a brilliant new product concept, or manufacturing may find the economies to make an infeasible product feasible. Innovation can happen anywhere.

- *Myth 4.* An innovation's technical superiority and strategic importance will guarantee acceptance.

  Interestingly enough, this is just not true. Timing—the matching of the readiness of the market with the availability of the useful product—is perhaps the single most important factor in commercial success or failure.

- *Myth 5.* The best way to inform others of the significance of your research is to describe the results in a paper. The irrefutable logic of your argument will convince them to adopt the new technology.

  How wrong can you be?! Some people read the literature and some don't. The people who can most effect your success probably do not. It may feel good to write a paper about what you've done, and it may enhance your research reputation, but there's lots more to esablishing significance than the printed page.

- *Myth 6.* The best way to build an effective research lab is to hire the best and brightest scientists available.

  Well, yes, to a point. But the scientists should understand the principle of research relevance. And they should understand how to bridge the gap to practice. Those traits aren't necessarily present in the traditional definition of the "best and the brightest."

- *Myth 7.* If you build a better mousetrap, the world will beat a path to your door.

  Sure—but only *if* the world knows about your mousetrap, what it's good for, and where your door is.

O'Brien's conclusion? That research must be supplemented with a marketing perspective. Researchers need to

- establish links to the wider world

- identify needs to serve as a basis for research studies
- sell ideas that result from their investigations
- transfer the results of their investigations to the needy
- foster technology transfer through their organizational design

That may not result in terribly "pure" research. But it is much more likely to lead to research that gets results. Do the researchers in *your* company take this point of view?

Software Learning: A New Source of Information

Where do you look if you want to learn something about software? There are several good answers to that question.

For one thing, you can look in the textbooks that are beginning to abound on the topic. There are general books on software engineering by people like Roger Pressman and Richard Fairley that are excellent. There are supurb anecdotal books like *The Mythical Man-Month* by Fred Brooks and *Peopleware* by DeMarco and Lister. There are masterful specialty books, like *The Art of Software Testing* by Glenford Myers. At long last, good material is becoming available.

For another thing, there are the journals. *System Development* does a good job of keeping managers of data processing informed. *Software—Practice and Experience*, which comes out of England, is especially good at covering the practitioner as well as the theoretical world. So does the journal I edit, *Journal of Systems and Software*, which is published by Elsevier in New York. Then there are the ACM and IEEE journals, like *Communications of the ACM*, and *IEEE Transactions on Software Engineering*, and *IEEE Software*. ACM even has a special interest group in software engineering, and it publishes a feisty little unrefereed journal called *Software Engineering Notes,* which in some ways is the best of the bunch.

Then, of course, there are the courses. If you're like me, you get more mail telling you about seminars and courses than you're able to keep up with. It would be nice if we had a *Consumer Reports* type analysis of the play-for-pay courses, but unfortunately none exists. You "pays your money and you takes your chances" seems to pretty well cover what you'll get here. Some of the seminar speakers are excellent and have excellent material, and some are not and do not.

But there is a new source of software-relevant material. It's the series of curriculum modules produced at the Software Engineering Institute in Pittsburgh. These modules each contain an in-depth nugget of information about some facet of the software world, complete with references to additional material, and they make a good place for a reasonably sophisticated reader to start learning about a particular software topic. And the best part is, they're free!

What is a curriculum module? Well, the Software Engineering Institute, among its other jobs, is trying to provide material to educators to help them teach software topics. A curriculum module is the delivery system for doing that. It tells an educator, in 15 to 45 pages, what the important topics are on a particular subject area, and where to go to find out more.

For educators, you say? And you're not an educator?

Well, although these modules are written with academic professors or industry trainers in mind, there's no reason why *you* can't get a copy of a module as your own source for learning more about a particular software-relevant topic. For instance, suppose you're interested in requirements and systems analysis. The SEI has these curriculum modules relevant to that topic:

- *Requirements Specification Overview.* Discusses the user and his or her needs. Covers application domains by category. Presents models of computation, such as state machines and computational graphs.
- *Formal Specification of Software.* Defines what formal specifications are, and the principles that underlie the concept. Discusses examples of formal specifications, and the process of creating them.
- *Software Specification: A Framework.* Exposes the ambiguity in the term *specification.* Presents the kinds of specifications that a software specialist might write. Describes how to assess specifications.

In addition, a relevant curriculum module currently being prepared is:

- *Requirements Analysis.* A practical look at the tasks associated with obtaining the requirements for a software system.

And another one for which authors are currently being sought is:

- *Specification Languages.* A look at specific formal specification languages, how to use them, and what they are good for.

From this, you can probably see that a curriculum module is not so much a broad look at a software topic such as you would see as a course in a college or a professional seminar, but a more intense look at a narrower software topic that one might use in conjunction with other curriculum modules to put together a course or seminar. The result is you can read one module to get a view of a particular narrow software topic, or a collection of modules to get a look at a broader topic in perspective.

With this view of a curriculum module in mind, here is the current menu of Software Engineering Institute curriculum modules, with more being created all the time: Requirements Specification Overview; Introduction to Software Design; The Software Technical Review Process; Software Configuration Management; Information Protection; Software Safety; Assurance of Software Quality; Formal Specification of Software; Unit Testing and Analysis; Models of Software Evolution: Life Cycle and Process; Software Specification: A Framework; Software Metrics; Introduction to Software Verification and Validation; and Intellectual Property Protection for Software. The breadth of the topics is limited only by the scope of the profession.

You may be wondering who writes these modules. Usually college professors or industry experts. Sometimes the best qualified people in the business. For example, Prof. Nancy Leveson of the University of California at Irvine wrote the module on Software Safety. She probably knows more about software safety than anyone. Prof. Pamela Samuelson of the University of Pittsburgh, a lawyer, wrote the module on Intellectual Property Protection for Software. Other work she has done on software and the law has resulted in important recent changes to government procurement policies for software. The chances are the module you're interested in will have been written by someone you've heard of.

So what's the catch, you may be wondering. These are free modules, written by the best in the business, and you can have them for the asking? Well, the answer is, there really isn't much of a catch. The Software Engineering Institute is government funded, so its materials must be given away. Oh, the modules are a little computer science-y, so they're sometimes more theoretical and obtuse than a practitioner might prefer. But if you can get past that, they're a new source—and a good one—for learning about software.

If you want to know more, for instance, to get a complete list of the modules available at any point in time, get in touch with Allison Brunvand, Software Engineering Institute, Carnegie-Mellon University, Pittsburgh PA 15213.

An Open Letter to
Computer Science Professors

This chapter is written as an open letter to a composite computer science professor from someone who is a composite practicing software maintainer. But its audience is really two entirely different kinds of people: those practitioners who want to learn a little more about the importance of software maintenance in the overall scheme of software things, and those computer science educators who fail to understand the importance of software maintenance in the broader computer science picture.

No matter which of those categories fits you, I hope you will enjoy my deeply-felt message.

Dear Computer Science Professor:

You did a wonderful job of teaching me everything you knew about computer science. About programming language features, and about data structure choices, and about algorithms and the big O, and about operating systems and compilers, and even a little about software engineering . . .

Well, surprise! Now that I am a professional software engineer, maintenance is what I am doing. And I wish I had been better prepared . . .

Now I realize, dear computer science professor, that you think there is nothing unique about maintenance . . . that in teaching us about develop-ment, you think you taught us everything there was to know. I've asked other computer science professors, and they feel the same way!

But you were wrong. There is *so* much to learn about software mainte-nance, and I am still doing a lot of learning. Let me tell you about the kinds of things I have learned.

Design for Maintenance

There is information about how to build software that's more maintainable—the job the developers do on behalf of the maintainers, the job that at the very least you should have told me about in your classes.

For example, there are a couple of key ideas all developers should learn such as to use the principle of *single-point control,* and to use the principle of *defensive design.*

Single-point control is an idea that you touched on, although you never called it that. Single-point control is the idea that anything that is done in multiple places in a program or its documentation or its data should be done in one place, then referenced in the other places. Examples of single-point control are

- *Modularity.* All of the reasons for modular programming that you *did* teach us are just instances of the generic concept, single-point control.
- *Data abstraction.* Again, all of the reasons for the idea of separating off data declarations and the operations on the data (which again you *did* teach us about) so that they can be cleanly referenced and revised are a part of single-point control.
- *Object orientation.* Same story all over again. You taught us about this, the idea of data abstraction with inheritance of the traits, but you didn't tie it in to either single-point control or maintenance.
- *Table and file driven design.* If the data of a program are centralized then when they inevitably change, the changes are limited to the data declarations, not the procedural references to them.
- As they say in the marketing world, "lots, lots more." Single-point control comes up in so many guises. Named data constants are an example, and so are normalized data bases, and so is good documenta-tion structure.

Defensive design is an idea you barely touched on. Defensive design is the collection of things the developer can do to make the software recover from the problems it encounters, rather than relying on the maintainer to do the recovery. Examples of defensive design are:

- *Exception handling.* I've learned that a lot of software (often over 50 percent) addresses the problems that shouldn't normally arise when the software is running, but will occasionally. These exception handlers, blocks of code that detect and react to faulty data and other anticipatable circumstances, are a major part of the developer's job.
- *Assertions.* Software can check itself as it runs, not just for anticipatable exceptions, but also for hardware or software faults. Assertions are simply built-in error checks with remedial sections of code to handle assertion-detected problems.
- *Overengineering.* Software stuffed into a too small and too slow computer can take double the maintenance time of better planned code/machine systems. Software that aborts when 15 pieces of data are submitted to a 14-place table is a burden for the maintainer. The developer can anticipate future problems and plan for maintenance growth.
- *Fault tolerance.* Software inevitably fails sometimes, no matter how careful we are about error removal. There is a whole collection of techniques that can be used if software must not fail. That collection is called *fault tolerance,* and involves diversity and redundancy in very special ways.

Doing Maintenance

But the specialized learning about software maintenance isn't limited to things the *developers* can do, dear computer science professor. There are unique things *maintainers* must do also.

For example, in the tools world, there are whole new collections of tools built just to help the maintainer. There are so many, people have begun to invent categories for them, and in fact the United States General Services Administration has selected a set of off-the-shelf tools which it calls "The Programmers Workbench." These are seen as the tools to "improve productivity in software management," especially software maintenance.

The tools categories are:

- Dependency analysis. Tools like cross-reference listers, call structure analyzers, data name standardizers, and ripple effect detectors that automatically produce tables of information of value to the maintainer in understanding the software being maintained.
- Reverse engineering. Tools like "undesigners," metrics analyzers, and performance analyzers help extract the underlying meaning and function found below the surface of a program's normal documentation.
- Program change analysis. These are tools like comparators, configuration management, and change reporting that help the maintainer manage changes to software under maintenance.

- Reconstruction. Tools like structuring engines, reformatters, and conditional compilers help the maintainer put the pieces of a software product back together again after the maintenance change has been made.

Managing Maintenance

Well, dear computer science professor, those topics just scratch the surface of the *technology* of maintenance. But in addition to that, there are some unique things one ought to know about managing maintenance.

For example, how should one *organize* the management function? Not just "should development and maintenance be in separate organizations?" (and incidentally, there's no correct generic answer to that one). But there are also such issues as:

- Who is responsible for deciding what changes are to be made, and when? (Answer: the *change board*.)
- Who is responsible for product testing and release decisions? (Answer: often, an organization called *product test*.)
- Who makes sure that the product doesn't get inconsistently changed, or irrevocably lost? (Answer: *configuration management*.)

You see, dear computer science professor? There are whole classes of organizations that are uniquely needed to do maintenance.

And there's more. I know that we didn't study a whole lot about people in computer science, dear professor, but there are people-oriented considerations that are vital to software maintenance.

For instance, some people aren't very good at doing maintenance. They can't innovate within the constraints of an existing program design, or they choose not to. They try to revise code without understanding the totality of the program. They aren't very patient, flexible, or analytic, and they aren't very good at thinking like someone else (the developer, for instance). The result is you can't just take the green and the dull and assign them to do software maintenance—it's a special and unique challenge all its own.

In fact, Bill Gates, a famous computer science person in his own right (he's the founder and head of Microsoft) sees maintenance techniques as the best way to learn computer science. He is quoted in *Programmers at Work*(*) as saying ". . . the best way to prepare [to be a programmer] is to write programs and to study great programs that other people have written . . . I went to the garbage cans at the Computer Science Center and I

*by Susan Lammers, published by Microsoft Press

fished out listings of their operating system," he says, recollecting how *he* learned to program during his days in college.

Champions of the Living Software

I've now rubbed shoulders with some of the top maintainers in the business (some people refer to them as "Champions of the Living Software"), dear computer science professor, at places like the Software Maintenance Association annual conference. (People go there who actually like to live and breathe software maintenance!) And I've learned that companies that really understand the importance of software maintenance go out on some interesting limbs to make the maintainers happy. They and their companies tend to do several important things:

- They see their roles clearly. The maintainer is more than a fixer; the maintainer, in fact, spends most of his or her time enhancing and improving.
- They see their roles as important. They keep the key software of the company functioning. That software is often the keys to the company, the underlying control of the company's future, and it is certainly the image of the company to the software's customers.
- They receive rewards when they do well. Some companies have given top maintenance achievers trinkets and mementos (gift certificates, plaques, free lunches) or career perks (special job titles like "applications support team leader," or clerical support for the less interesting tasks), or corporate belief ("the best and the brightest are in maintenance.")
- They use the new tools and techniques I told you about earlier.
- They are carefully tied in with their users (with such techniques as user groups, user newsletters, user advisory boards, or user surveys).

And they see one thing as most important overall—the quality of the software product, not the cost of the service, comes first. The task of these maintainers, as they see it, is to prolong the life of the system, and as professionals that is what they devote their efforts to.

Educate the Educators

So, dear computer science professor, I have decided it is time to educate the educators. I think you need to know that maintainers

- Spend 40 percent to 80 percent of the software dollar

- Spend 75 percent of their time improving on products, and only 15 percent fixing them (one maintenance wag, Richard K. Ball, said in his Software Maintenance News column in 1988, "The role of the software maintainer is not to fix the mistakes of others. We fix bugs as a courtesy.")
- Support people who control our economic system, and build products of more advanced technology than our parents ever dreamed of, and in fact sent spacecraft to other planets.

I am, in fact, *proud* to be a maintainer, dear computer science professor. It's not just that I feel good about what I do. The world in general is beginning to see the importance, as well.

The Wall Street Journal, in a front-page article in 1988, said that we are "vital" and that our job is to "ride to the rescue."

IBM, in a 1980 research report, said "The maintenance . . . problem is now the central issue of software engineering."

And Barry Boehm, one of software engineering's leading spokesmen, said in a 1987 keynote address "Raise the maintenance function to a high-prestige position."

There *are* significant skills required for what we maintainers do. There *is* information we need to do our jobs. We *are* important in the overall scheme of things.

Can you, dear computer science professor, work with us to help produce people with the information and skills that are needed in a field as critical as ours?

I think you can. I hope you can. But I know that, unless there is a change in both your thinking and your action, you will not.

According to the same IBM research report in 1980, "Software engineering is polarized around two subcultures: the speculators and the doers. The former invent but do not go beyond publishing novelty, hence never learn about the idea's usefulness—or lack of it. The latter, not funded for experimentation but for efficient product development, must use proven, however antiquated, methods."

Well, dear computer science professor, us doers of the world need the help of you speculators. I hope you will see fit to help us.

A Postmortem of the Battleground

How Can Computer Science Truly Become a Science, and Software Engineering Truly Become Engineering?

I want to kick around a couple of software-related words with you here.

The words are *formal* and *structured*.

Those words are adjectives, often tacked on the front of such nouns as *specification languages* and *documentation*. They are generally considered to be positive adjectives; that is, a formal or structured something or other is thought to be better than the same something or other without formality or structure.

What is interesting about these two words is that there is a body of computing people behind each of them. Behind the word *formal* tends to be a large part of the academic education community. Behind the word *structured* tends to be a large part of the entrepreneurial education community. In those communities, especially, those words take on profound meaning.

The question I want to ask here is the heretical question *"Should* these words take on profound meaning?" What do we really know about things that are formal and things that are structured?

Well, we know that they are supported by a lot of advocacy. That is, whenever you see anything written on "Formal Poobah" or "Structured Gizmo" you know in advance that the tone of the article will be positive, perhaps even laudatory. "Formal/structured Gizbah should be required learning for all computing practitioners" is not an unusual position for such an article to take. Neither is "We trained all our people to employ Formal/structured Poomo and our productivity is up eleventy-six percent."

Now I want to ask a question. The question is "How do we know that formal/structured whatever is better than nonformal/structured whatever?"

Seems like a silly question, right? I mean, intuitively things that use those positive adjectives are going to be better than things that don't. Right?

Well, I suppose the correct answer is "yes." "Yes, it does seem intuitively that those things would be better." But the key word here is *intuitively*. Is intuitively really the best way to make decisions about what moves we make in trying to get our software practice to be more productive?

Now that the question has been asked and answered, let me make a point.

In the science of computer science and the engineering of software engineering, there is no strong experimental component.

That is, we shouldn't *have* to rely on intuition to decide whether formal/structured approaches are better than "un" ones. We should have scientifically defined and conducted experiments which could give us quantitative answers to questions like that. Then we could make statements like "structured design has been shown to be an X% improvement over unstructured design," or "software that has been formally verified has been shown to be Y% more reliable than software which has not."

And based on those kinds of statements, we could do a cost-benefit analysis of whether it was worth putting $Z,000 worth of training courses in front of our people to upgrade old knowledge into new. After all, not all new knowledge is better than old knowledge. How can we tell the difference?

So why don't we already have an experimental component to our field's science and our field's engineering? There are two reasons that I can think of:

1. Experiments that are properly controlled and conducted are hard and expensive to conduct. It's not enough to rope three undergraduate students into writing 50 lines of Basic and then compare notes. If an experiment is going to be meaningful, it ought to involve real software developers solving real software problems in a carefully predefined and measured setting.

2. The engineers and scientists in our field are neither motivated nor prepared to conduct meaningful experiments. Advocacy has been with us for so long that it just doesn't seem to occur to anyone that there's a component missing from our research. And without motivation to supply the missing component, no one is getting the proper intellectual tools to know how to conduct experimental research.

(Perhaps the words *no one* in the preceding paragraph is an example of going too far. For example, the folks working on the intersection of software and psychology, the "empirical studies" folks, are doing fairly interesting experimental work.)

So how do we solve the problem of getting good experimental work? Since it's not going to be cheap or easy, unfortunately, the solution has to be a "solution in the large." We need a national institute, funded by major industry or the government, with enough resources to do this kind of thing. Or a private company with enough startup resources to conduct the experiments and then market the results to industrial targets.

You may be thinking "we already have such a place." Isn't that what the Software Productivity Consortium and the Software Engineering Institute are supposed to be doing, for example? Well, yes, it seems to me that they should be doing that, but the fact of the matter is that they're not. Experimentation is hard and costly, and most people would rather do "thought" research than experimental research. The industry and government-funded institutions that could be doing experimental research simply are not doing it, and are unlikely to start.

But wouldn't it be nice if they did? Wouldn't it be nice if someone with the needed resources would start something like the *Software Consumer Reports?* Then we could begin moving what David Parnas calls the "folklore" of computing into something more scientific. And then, with experimental results in hand, we wouldn't wonder any more about the merits of adjectives like *formal* and *structured*. We would know not only what they were about, but what they were worth to us.

Wouldn't that be nice? Important, even?

My Trivial/Brilliant Concept Called "Problem Solving"

This is an essay about "problem solving." In it, I'm going to say some things that are either trivial or brilliant, and to tell you the truth I don't know which they are. Could *you* help me figure it out?

It seems to me that the business we're in, way deep down, is *not* data processing or computing or any of those technology-oriented things we usually say we're doing.

The business we're in is problem solving.

But that's really a trivial idea, of course, because almost everyone is in the business of problem solving. If you're in personnel, you solve people problems. If you're in manufacturing, you solve assembly problems. If you're in accounting, you solve financial problems. Problem solving, in fact, is a universal endeavor. We just happen to be different because we use computers to solve the problems we deal with.

So where does the brilliance enter into this trivial idea?

Well, take a look at the advice we give to people who have problems to solve. We tell them to get the problem defined. We tell them to plan a solution. We tell them to build the solution. We tell them to check the solution. And we tell them, if necessary, that once the solution is working they need to keep the solution working.

We give them this advice whether they're learning technical communication and composing a short article, or whether they're learning mathematics and they're attacking a story problem, or whether they're learning architecture and are designing a building. In fact, we seem to tell them this no matter what the problem is they're solving!

What seems to me to be true, then, is that there's a general approach to problem solving that's independent of the application domain it falls in.

Now, what makes this interesting and perhaps even brilliant is that what we just defined a couple of paragraphs back is what we software folk think we invented decades ago. In the late 1960s we invented the "software life cycle." In this life cycle, we say we define the requirements for our computing problem, we design a solution, we code the design, we test the code, and we maintain the final product. Now tell me—how do these life-cycle activities compare with those problem-solving activities? They're almost item-by-item identical.

In other words, what we call the software life cycle is not a new idea at all. And it's not our software idea, either. It's an idea that comes from a discipline broader and more important than ours.

Let's return to the implications of that in a minute. First, though, I want to identify a couple of ironies.

The first irony is we software folk spend a lot of time debating what life cycle we should use. Some people have rejected the whole idea of the life cycle, saying that it is "harmful." Others say that with new ideas like prototyping, the old life cycle simply doesn't work. New life cycles have been proposed. The Software Engineering Institute, where I used to work, published a report defining more than a half dozen of them.

What's the irony here? It's that we've missed a key point. The life cycle, that generalized problem-solving approach, isn't ours to reject. It's an interdisciplinary notion, and one that we can refine for software purposes. But rejecting it, or radically changing it, is rejecting the problem-solving wisdom of much older disciplines than ours.

The second irony is some software people never really understood this life cycle. Once it was "discovered," some people took it as an ironclad set of rules, a process that had to be used to build software solutions, an inviolate approach that had to be followed in just the right order and in just the right way. You cannot start design until the requirements are complete. You cannot start coding until the design is complete. You cannot start testing until the code is complete.

That rigid view of the life cycle should have flown in the face of our common sense. That technical writer we mentioned earlier, who learns for example to plan the writing before actually writing it, nevertheless knows that a little trial writing can go a long way toward firming up a plan, and that a wadded up page of manuscript that failed to pass checkout may simply mean that the problem was not quite yet understood or the plan was not quite right. That architect we mentioned before who designed buildings before building them actually knows that you build a model of the final building and tinker with it to understand the problem and its planned solution before finishing the plan and pouring the concrete. Nobody, nobody ever insisted that the steps in problem solving had to be done only in the proper sequence before. Where did we software folk get such a crazy idea?

But to leave these ironies behind, and proceed . . .

I am becoming more and more convinced that there is a general discipline of problem solving out there in the world somewhere, and that we software folks are busily rediscovering it, step by clumsy step.

If that is true, then there may be more wisdom out there that we have not yet "invented," but which we will invent at great expense and stare at with much wonder and misinterpret with much ignorance. And what a shame that will be, because this wisdom may be available for our plucking, if we only knew what tree it grows on.

I haven't pursued this idea academically, so I don't know if there is an academic discipline that claims the topic of problem solving. I certainly was never exposed to one in college. But if there isn't there certainly should be. Not imbedded in engineering or science or architecture or mathematics, however, where only the favored few can find it. But out there in the open, in what some schools call the interdisciplinary core, where everybody gets exposed to the idea. Problem solving, as we saw earlier, is or should be everybody's interest area.

So let me leave you with a couple of questions. Is this idea of mine as trivial as it sometimes seems to me, or is it as brilliant as it seems to me at other times?

And, perhaps more importantly, is there anywhere in the academic world where problem solving is presently taught, a place we could go to anticipate the next great discovery of software engineering wisdom?

If you have an answer to either question, I'd love to hear from you.

Software Failure:
Why Does it Happen?

Over the years, I've become an expert on software failure. I'm an Association for Computing Machinery national lecturer on failure. I've written a collection of books on failure, like *The Universal Elixir and Other Computing Projects Which Failed,* and *Computing Catastrophes.* I've even become so steeped in failure that I still own a Studebaker, and I believe that Jimmy Carter was one of our finest presidents!

However, when I look at failure I like to look at it from a fun point of view. Software people love to swap failure stores; I've just formalized that into a public process. I believe that when we can laugh, first with someone else who has failed, and later on at our own failings, we have gotten in touch with a vitally important piece of our personal humanity and humility.

But as time has gone by in my little failure-for-fun world, some members of my listening and reading audience have urged me to explore the more important, more visible failures of the computing world, and to try to extract learning experiences from them. After all, the child learns most indelibly from the hand it places on the hot stove. Here, I will try to Get Serious About Failure.

When I look around at the littered remains of the projects I've talked about and written about for fun, I see a few patterns forming, a few common causes for those failures. It is those patterns that I will talk about here.

Inability to estimate

The first and most pervasive cause I see for failures in the software field is our inability to estimate. No matter how hard we try, no matter how many good tools and algorithms we use, our cost and schedule estimates are badly out of touch with the reality that emerges when the product is at last completed. In one of the most recent and spectacular examples, Microsoft misestimated how long it would take to bring out a new version of its word processor, removed the previous version from the marketplace before the new one was ready, and saw its stock value fall 15 percent in one day. Other software houses promise software so long before it is ready that the whole industry is slapped with the expression "vaporware," meaning a product announced so early that it has all the reality of a puff of smoke.

Why do we do so badly at estimation? Probably because we still don't understand this infant field of ours. We're still barely grasping the fact that there's a lot more to writing software than coding. We're still barely grasping the fact that checkout takes a lot longer than we ever dreamed, and that the process is unpredictable. We're still reeling under the reality that maintenance consumes more than half of most people's software dollar. The problem isn't so much that we don't know how to build the software product—I think we do. The problem is that we still don't quite understand the process.

Why does it matter that our estimates are so bad? Because we are trying to manage to them. We set up budgetary frameworks and intricate schedules based on our estimates, and then we try to get the software developers to deliver product when the framework says product will be delivered. And when the product is *not* delivered then, we put management pressure on to minimize the amount of delay between the scheduled completion date and the ever-changing *real* one. That, in turn, exacerbates the problem. Slowly we turn a late, overbudget project into a late, overbudget and unreliable one by skimping on the testing processes so necessary to getting the bugs out. I personally believe that the "software crisis," the saying that software is "always over budget, behind schedule, and unreliable," is almost single-handedly caused by poor estimation. If that is so, then this is clearly the most important problem in software engineering.

There are lots of people trying to help. Algorithms for estimation abound. Some of them have been coded into software. But the performance of the algorithmic estimation approaches is as erratic as the human estimations are optimistic. Various studies have shown that algorithmic estimates vary by as much as 800 percent for the same hypothetical software project. Algorithms may be the answer some day, perhaps even today for you in your software shop if you've tweaked a model to meet your needs and validated it against your reality, but they are not really here in any reliable way for the software masses yet.

So we continue to use human estimation techniques, for all their subjectivity and optimism, because the skilled software person is still our best source of predictions about the future. But we fail in general to do the one thing we *can* do now to begin to whittle away at our ignorance or our process. We fail to collect historic data describing the past realities of software construction that we might be able to use to make more accurate estimations about our future. Carefully selected and collected historic data relating *processes* to *personnel levels and durations* to *application and complexity domains* will go a long way to giving each computing shop control over its own estimation destiny. But all too few companies are doing it.

There is another interesting problem with estimation practices in software. Those who have peeked over the fence at our related disciplines say that nobody, *nobody*, tries to do a final estimate as early in the development process as we software folk. When do we typically produce our estimates? Usually before or during the requirements-gathering exercise. How can we possibly know enough to predict how long it will take to produce a product when we still haven't wrapped our arms around the problem yet? Perhaps we are living and dying by estimates that we should never have been tied to in the first place. It is almost as if software people, the new kids on the political block, are being picked on by the bullies in our related system disciplines, being cajoled into making promises that *they* would never make, and we are too new, too ignorant, and too gutless to stand up to them. Perhaps the *real* answer to the software estimation problem is progressive estimation, with a new estimate produced at each of several clearly identified milestones, and with all decision making being based on the *latest*, not the *earliest*, estimate. That exercise in reality may leave managers who need control feeling that they have lost that control, but then in today's world of estimation and reality that feeling of control is only an illusion anyway.

But, you may say, if estimates are allowed to change, won't technical people take advantage of that? There are some interesting data that relate to that question. According to one study, software people who build software under *no* schedule constraints are more productive than those who build software to a schedule, no matter who determined the schedule (even when they determined it themselves). It is as if, and some key software people take this position, people are at their most productive when *they* retain control over their work. It's something to think about.

Unstable requirements

The second most common cause of failure, I believe, is the instability of the requirements we work to. All too often we find ourselves shooting at a moving target. In the attempt to be nice guys, we buy into changes the customer or user wants that pervert our design process and decimate our schedules.

No one can solve any problem where the nature of the problem is changing. Not software people, not anyone. But because software is soft and thus malleable, the world believes and we attempt to prove that we can produce products so flexible that changes don't matter much.

And we fail. Again and again, we demonstrate that for all the softness of software, it is not so soft as to be flexibly free. The best way to see this is in looking at software maintenance. What is software maintenance? Predominantly, making changes to the software to meet new requirements. That costs from 40 to 80 percent of the software dollar. Software may be soft—we are indeed able to produce more flexible solutions than almost any other discipline—but it is not so soft that change is free. Far from it, in fact. Change is the biggest moneymaker in the software world!

The secret of unstable requirements, then, is simply the acknowledgment of reality. Freeze the requirements at the outset of the project, right after the approval of the requirements specification. Don't be hard-nosed about having done so—nobody wants to be frozen into a solution that changing perceptions indicate won't work. But when the inevitable change requests come along, get a good conservative estimate of their impact (see the number one failure problem mentioned earlier!) and then charge the customer for doing it. If the customers want it badly enough, they'll pay. If they don't, then aren't you glad you didn't make the change for nothing?!

Probably as recently as five years ago, I believed that unstable requirements were the number one problem in software. It is an indication of our evolving political and technical maturity that it has slid (at least in my perception) to number two. Most software people understand the message of this problem. It is acting on it, rather than understanding it, that allows the problem to persist in this number two position.

It is interesting to note, however, that the current high-tech approaches to requirements (formal methods and formally defined requirements languages) are addressing a rather different part of the requirements problem. Adding rigor to unstable requirements gives us rigorous unstable requirements—a situation no better than unstable unrigorous requirements. The solution to requirements instability will not come from the research and technical world. It is solely a management problem.

Fads and fallacies

That brings us to our third most important cause of failure. This problem, the one I call fads and fallacies, is one that I simply don't understand. That is, I understand what it is; I just don't understand why it persists.

To put it bluntly, some people in software still believe in the silver bullet. If you haven't read Fred Brooks's paper about silver bullets, let me explain briefly. Software is seen as being analagous to a werewolf, a problem grown so serious that we must slay it. But only silver bullets, according to legend, can slay the werewolf. So we must look for the imaginary silver bullet in order to destroy the mythical werewolf.

Well, whatever you believe about the software crisis, it is certainly not as mythical as the werewolf. But more to the point, it is hopeless to seek an imaginary solution to a problem, no matter how real (or mythical) the problem is.

In this analogy, what do we mean by a silver bullet? A breakthrough that will somehow make it possible to painlessly and cheaply build software. And what is the problem with silver bullets? I would assert, as does Fred Brooks, that there simply aren't any left to find.

Then why is the search for the silver bullet a failure-causing problem? Because the search for magic solutions diverts us from the more important search for mundane ones. It is all right for researchers in ivy-covered halls to look for silver bullets (although it would be nice if some researchers also looked for more promising solutions). It is not all right when managers of real-live software projects neglect available solutions and instead invest in the hope that magic ones will arrive.

What evidence do I have that this is so? Here are several examples.

First, take the "structured programming revolution." It burst on us all in the 1970s, and before we knew what was happening thirty dozen consultants were making gallons of money training all the programmers in the world in doing it. Never mind that there were no experimental findings which could tell us the benefits of doing that. Never mind that cooler heads said that structured programming was what good programmers had been doing all along. Never mind that when the smoke cleared away and we did get visibility, it appeared to be true that the productivity and quality benefits, clearly there, were down in the 5 percent to 10 percent level (depending on how ugly the earlier "spaghetti code" was). A lot of energy, time, and money was poured into making us all structured programmers. Was that really the best use of that energy, time, and money?

For an answer to that question, consider the source language debugger, the tool that allows programmers to check out code in the same language that they write it in. As early as the 1950s, programmers had access to high-level languages, and all the productivity and quality improvements those breakthroughs brought with them. As early as the 1960s, tool builders were building source debuggers, obsoleting the machine-code debug tools still prevalent in the business. But when did source language debuggers come into heavy productive use? Not until the late 1970s, fully ten years after the technology was known and available. I think it is no accident of timing that the structured programming revolution was happening when the breakthrough of source language debugging was waiting in the wings. In the search for a silver bullet, we missed a less exciting but more useful capability.

But that's in the past, you say? We wouldn't make that mistake in the enlightened 1990s? *Wrong!* There's another technology waiting in the wings today just as source language debugging did a couple of decades ago, and decision makers are studiously ignoring it. What is this technology? The test coverage analyzer.

What is a test coverage analyzer for? It measures how thoroughly your test cases cover the structure of the program under test. Why should we care? Because testing to assure that all the requirements for a software product are met is simply not enough. It is necessary, for reasons too complex to go into here, to test structural components as well as requirements satisfaction.

Why are test coverage analyzers not in common use in the workplace? It's the same story as source language debug. In spite of the fact that the technology has been known for over a decade, and in spite of the fact that there are products for a variety of environments solidly in place (including some that run on microcomputers), few software shops are using them. They are not using them because

1. There is little glamour in "back-end" life-cycle tools. Management has been sold on the benefits of "front-end loading" (as well it should), and has lost interest in the grubbier and more difficult back-end process, such as checkout.
2. Researchers and hucksters keep telling management what it wants to hear, that breakthrough solutions—silver bullets—are out there just waiting to be used.

I said earlier that I don't really understand this phenomenon. Why do software managers, people who get measured by their ability to produce real software on schedule and within budget, keep reaching for silver bullets and ignoring more meaningful, more available solutions? I don't have an answer to that. It just doesn't make sense to me. The only thing I can figure is that there seem to be more rewards in our fast-changing field for the person who speaks the latest technology, no matter how unreal it is, than there are for the person who speaks mundane reality.

In fact, this whole dilemma, which I call "fads and fallacies" because of a tendency of people to follow a new idea blindly into a box canyon, has produced strange bedfellows. On the side of the latest technologies are the researchers, the commercial hucksters, and the fad-following managers. Other than an interest in what is new, these people have very little in common!

There is a great deal of suppressed emotion attached to these fads and fallacies issues. Take proof of correctness, the notion that it will be possible to mathematically prove that software is correct. Twice in recent history the advocates of this silver bullet and its opponents have clashed in ugly outbursts in the pages of the leading professional journals, the latest beginning with the March 1989 issue of the flagship publication of the Association for Computing Machinery, the *Communications of the ACM*. These are not simply calm and reasoned professional differences. Names are being called, and personal integrity is geing questioned. Why is the emotion so intense? I would assert that part of the reason is the pent-up frustration of those who see more available solutions passed over in favor of silver bullet promises. As long as fads and fallacies prevail over realism, I believe that the potential for these emotional outbursts will continue.

And, more importantly, I believe that one of the most serious problems in software will persist.

An overview

So where have we been in this trip through software failure-land? We have seen three of the most serious software failure causes—inability to estimate, unstable requirements, and fads and fallacies.

Are there solutions to these problems? Perhaps, although failure causers of this magnitude are not easily corrected (if they were, they would have been!).

For inability to estimate, solutions are

- Gathering historic data to improve our future estimates
- Analyzing the estimation process to see if incremental estimates would give a better handle on reality, consistent with the approaches of other disciplines.

For unstable requirements, the solution is simply making sure that

- customers pay realistically for any requirements changes they want. For fads and fallacies, solutions are

- Convincing managers who have had their hands burned by researcher and huckster promises that there are better sources of wisdom to listen to

- Finding someone, *someone,* to establish a National Software Experiment Center where the fads and fallacies can be explored experimentally before the practitioners of the land follow them blindly into those box canyons.

There are no easy solutions, just as there are no silver bullets. Perhaps it is simply knowing what the most serious problems are that will help us all begin to find solutions to them.

The Importance of the
Application Domain Cluster

Let me make a prediction about the future of software engineering.

By the turn of the century, software engineering will have split into multiple disciplines. Just as there is electrical engineering, mechanical engineering, and civil engineering, there will be scientific software engineering, business software engineering, real-time software engineering, and systems software engineering.

Why do I feel that way? Because I believe that we are just now beginning to grasp the importance of the application domain to how we build software. And I believe as we get a firmer grasp of the implications of that importance, we will begin to see that we cannot talk about software engineering without talking specifically about its constituent "application domain clusters," those topical areas that have similar problem characteristics in common.

The era we are passing through I would characterize as the era of "universal solutions." Advocates for languages, methodologies, and tools are making claims that their offerings are the best for solving *any* problems. Usually, these claims are wrong. Optimism born of ignorance has allowed experts in one application domain cluster to assume, and proclaim, that what they have learned will port into other domains. Usually, and unfortunately, it will not.

What evidence do I have for this trend?

1. At a Distinguished Lecture at the Software Engineering Institute in 1988, Victor Vyssotsky, director of the Digital Equipment Corporation Cambridge research lab, took as his theme this same idea, saying that the complications of the domain are as vital a part of the software engineer's toolbox as software knowledge itself.

2. At the International Conference on Software Engineering in 1987, one of the few times audience applause interrupted a presentation happened when John Kelly, speaking on real-time design methodologies, said that there was no best design approach for all applications, and that the search for one could get in the way of more important progress in the field.

3. When the Japanese hypothesized a national standard toolkit for software engineers and began defining what it should contain, the COBOL toolkit and the Fortran toolkit were given very different functional capabilities.

4. In spite of the early euphoria over 4GLs and their impact on software development, the use of these languages has penetrated only a few closely-related application domains.

5. Experiments in data and logic representation by Iris Vessey of Penn State have shown that the choice of representational schema should depend more on something called "cognitive fit," the fit of the tools to the task, than any other factor.

6. In the March 1989 *IEEE Transactions on Software Engineering*, Bo Sanden, in "The Case for Electric [sic] Design of Real-Time Software," argues for what he calls an "eclectic" approach to design, saying "rather than arguing about which design method is best, we should . . . use any combination of approaches that yields important results in a given situation, no matter from what methods they are taken."

7. In a survey of commercial data processing management about productivity factors conducted for the periodical System Development, "expertise in application" moved up from its 1984 ranking of fourth most important to its 1987 position of second (right behind "personnel/team capability").

8. In the Rich and Waters paper on the "cocktail party myth" of automated programming, one of the myths debunked was the thought that automatic programming need not know about the application domain.

9. In the Basili and Selby paper on testing versus reviews, the authors found a link between the application domain of the software and several error and error-removal characteristics of the software.

Now that I've said what I believe will happen and explained why I feel that way, I have to confess that I'm not all that confident of my prediction. I still see ample evidence of the persistence of the old approach. Advocates for new scientific languages recommend their use for business applications, never realizing that many features needed for such applications are simply not supported in any meaningful way by the new language. Claims for the universality of methodologies and CASE tools still are surrounded by application-independent hype. Data flow diagrams, clearly useful for representing processes in data-oriented applications but of arguable value for others, are still taught as *the* structured approach to software. Expectations of automated software development neglect the need for application expertise in addition to software expertise in the tools to do the automating. There is an entrenched belief system that will have to be overturned to make my prediction come true.

The first step in making my prediction come true, I believe, is the instigation of research efforts focused on this area. What are the important application domain clusters? What characterizes them? What functional needs should their programming languages support? What tools and methods could support those functional needs? How can we best teach about those functional needs? Where is the dividing line between universal approaches and domain approaches? How much of software engineering (and computer science, for that matter) can be presented in an application-independent manner?

The answers to these questions must come from those who understand the multiplicity of domain clusters and their needs. In other words, this is an area where practice leads theory, and theory building should include studies of practice. For example, a survey of practitioners to identify domain clusters, and primitives needed in particular domains, could be an important platform on which to build further research.

In the software engineering educational system of the future, where some of the things I've talked about here may come true, I see a partitioning of learning into topics like these:

In the universal core:
- P = problem solving (application-independent)

In the computing core:
- C = computer science topics (application-independent)

In the software engineering specialty:
- S = software engineering topics (application-independent)

In a software engineering degree program:
- SD = software engineering topics (application-dependent)
- AD = application domain specific topics

This educational process could then produce the following kinds of people:

- Computer science researchers (P + C + relevant AD)
- Software engineering researchers (P + C + S + relevant SD + relevant AD)
- Software systems specialists (P + C + S + relevant SD)
- Application domain software engineers (P + C + S + SD + AD)
- Application domain users (P + AD)

Prediction is, of course, a strange business. As Ed Yourdon points out, predictions about technology are always too conservative (technology moves faster and in more directions than we predict), but predictions about sociology are always too radical (society always moves more slowly than we predict). But still, I see some important factors in what I've said here that will cause change in the future. It will be interesting to see what that change will *really* be!

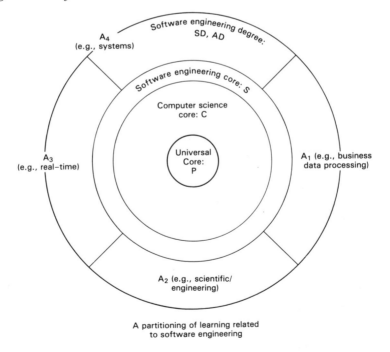

A partitioning of learning related
to software engineering

Can You Help Me Find It?

Fun. That's what software is all about, right? Those of us who eat, sleep and breathe computing and software do it because it's fun.

Oh, sure. We also do it for the money, the status, the professional advancement, and all those other mundane things that people write books about. But basically, we're in it for fun. That's why no one has ever written a book called *The One-Minute Programmer* . . . not because programming takes longer than that, but because who could ever quit after one minute?

Now that I've said that, though, I have a confession to make. Software *used to be* fun for me. After 30 years, it's not nearly as much fun any more. And as I work my way into my third mid-life crisis, I'm trying to figure out why. I'm writing this story to see if any of you readers out there can help me.

Here's where I've gotten so far. I've established some candidate explanations to try on for size.

1. *Employers think 30-year people are too valuable to let them program.*
   The last time anyone *really* asked me to write a program for money was so long ago I can't remember when. Oh, sure, I get to study

requirements, or write proposals, or do research, or write papers. But it's not the same. The fun in programming is programming. Nothing else really hacks it (cough). And employers believe that a fresh young programmer is just as good as an experienced older one.

2. *Programmers suffer burnout.*
   What's fun about programming is also what's awful about it. It's weaving a thousand tiny, intricate details into a functioning tapestry, an executable work of art. And after awhile, tangling with those details becomes less like fun and more like work. Why else would so many programmers aspire to become managers . . . what's the fun in that?

3. *The older you get, the more uptight you get.*
   Now *there's* a truly revolting thought! Have we learned so little about life, we experienced folk, that it becomes *more* of a burden as we live it, rather than *less*? Growing older should, in part, be a refinement of the ability to have fun. Looking about me at my age-peers, I don't believe I see that happening.

The list could be longer. That's one thing I'm counting on from you, dear reader. But let me wrap up this story by telling you what brought this issue to a focus.

I don't know how better to put this: I now have a second-generation programmer. Thirty years ago I had a son, and darned if he didn't decide to follow in his father's footsteps, cow pucky, program bugs, and all. So now there's a new generation programmer out there with my name on him. And as I watch his career progress, I see him having fun. Nostalgia and déjà vu . . . just like I used to.

It was his write-protect-ring story that got me. There he was, sitting around on a laid-back Friday afternoon at his particular employer's software factory, mellow after a week of hard work. And damned if one of the crew didn't throw a write-protect-ring at someone else (you know the write-protect-ring? The badly-named plastic gizmo that allows you to write on a tape when it's present, and protect it from writing when it's absent?). And, as will happen among spirited folk, the volley was returned. Write-protect-rings were flying through the air like bugs in an undebugged program. Even the corporate vice president got into the act (you know how small some of these contemporary software houses are, and how young their executives!). There was my son, a big smile on his face, happily telling me this story. And there was me-the-listener, analyzing my reaction and finally identifying it as *jealousy*. What was flashing through my mind was those halcyon days at the beginning of *my* career, when I swapped stories, shot rubber bands, and played ten-second chess on the job just like God intended us to do. So what happened?

What happened, indeed? I got more experienced. I got paid more. I got to feeling more responsible, somehow. I wrote some books, authored a column or two. I did research, wrote a paper or two. I got *successful*, just like All-American boys and girls are supposed to dream about.

But somewhere along the line, I think, I lost something. Can you help me find it?

An Ode to the
Software Young at Heart

Quite awhile back I wrote a column ("Can You Help Me Find It?") lamenting the problems of growing old in the software field. No, not the problems of physical age; the problems caused by the expectations of our society that we should grow more serious and become more managerial as we grow older.

To illustrate the point, I told the story of my son, now in the software business, and how on a Friday afternoon he and his peers sat around throwing write-protect-rings at each other for recreation. "Whatever happened to those fun times that I used to have?" I lamented. And I asked readers for input.

Well, input I got. Apparently the problem of growing old in a society and a system that expects certain things of older people struck a responsive chord. What I want to do here is excerpt the best of the comments. As you read them, imagine some background music, perhaps something I would call "An Ode to the Software Young at Heart." The music is cheery, not depressing, but there is a touch of sadness to it. Imagine, perhaps, Barbra Streisand's "Happy Days are Here Again," sprightly words sung at a dirge-like pace.

Perhaps Chris Torkildson of Eden Prairie, Minnesota, said it best:

> In the first ten years, my wife accused me of loving my work. She said no one who works for a salary should love their work. I always responded that anyone who didn't was doomed to a life of boredom. I don't think that I love my work anymore.

> I analyzed what happened during the days I came home feeling good as opposed to the other kind, and came up with the following conclusions:

> You feel good when you solve problems. In an intricate programming job you have thousands of problems, so many opportunities to feel good. As a programming manager you have many fewer problems, they're just much bigger. Not so much chance to solve them.

> You have fun when things move. Kids like fast bikes and roller coasters. Programmers like the upward evolution of their work. It makes you feel good when someone asks you for a change and you can do it in a couple of hours. With larger projects, you have a much harder time making things move. All of the steering committees, review committees, budget approvals, etc., cause things to move slowly . . .

> You feel good when the people you work with feel good. It is very exciting to work in a fast track programming environment with excellent programmers having a good time. As a manager you get the "policeman's syndrome" which means all you ever see are unhappy people . . .

Benjamin Doors of Villa Park, Illinois, also responded. Like Chris, he took an analytical look at the problem:

> Unfortunately, when you're a cog in a modern machine, it's hard to keep a sense of fun. Bureaucracies don't realize that some people like yourself have a concept of fun. Fun means experiencing the personal satisfaction of accomplishing a task; the comraderie of group effort; the joy of serendipitous discovery, and the application of this creativity to practical problems . . .

> Personally, I hope you're ready to trade a certain amount of success for fun.

But Willard (Bill) Holden of San José, California (a former ACM regional rep) got into the theme the most:

> Don't even look for it; as the saying goes, "You can't go back." Be realistic; industry doesn't want us old farts around, we cost too much. Also, if we lower our salary requirements they think that there must be something wrong with our work. We're in a no-win situation so we might as well accept the inevitable.

> Bob, the inevitable isn't so bad, either. Look at you, writing the only interesting column in a monthly periodical . . .

and then Bill went on to include a copy of an April Fool's letter he had sent to some friends, telling the story of his fantasized major life change:

> . . . She is now 22 and both intelligent and beautiful. We are to be married in June. As a wedding gift, we will receive a villa on a private Greek Island. We will also have a large, air conditioned apartment in Athens . . .

Now there's a man who knows how to fantasize! (I can almost hear the tempo of "Happy Days Are Here Again" picking up in the background!)

Thanks to everyone who responded. I may not be able to solve the problem (short of disappearing into a Bill Holden fantasy!), but I certainly understand it a lot better now.

What about you? Is software as much fun for you as it used to be? If it isn't, what are you doing about it? I'd love to get some more answers.

Epilog

Writing a collection of essays can be a dangerous endeavor.

First, the word *essay* itself is a putoff to most readers. In the nooks and crannies of our emotional history, it tends to mean "dry and dusty." I hope that these essays are not dry and dusty; they're not to me, but then what author was ever a fair judge of his or her own work?!

But more importantly, there is a question of nutrition. A collection of essays is wonderful to read a while and put down and pick up again on a rainy afternoon with a fire in the fireplace and a drink by your hand. (That's an experience I've had with Brooks's *The Mythical Man-Month*, DeMarco and Lister's *Peopleware*, and Weinberg's *Understanding the Professional Programmer*, and I've enjoyed it each time I've had it).

But the judgment comes when you finally put the book down at the end: did the verbal meal you just consumed have any lasting nutritional value? There is a danger, in a collection of essays, that you are left with the proverbial full feeling that goes away in an hour or two.

What, if anything, did I *really* say in this book? A reviewer challenged me to answer that question. Here is what I came up with. It is a distillation of the thoughts of the essays, organized as a collection of pithy quotes intended for a diverse target audience according to my perception of their nutritional needs. There is a danger here. These pithy thoughts, coming as they do at the end of the meal, may be the tastes you remember rather than the more elaborately prepared essays themselves.

But so be it. In the interests of tatting up, and given that our society is well into fast food, here is a quick summation of the meal we have just shared.

May the meal proper—and these taste bites—not leave you with indigestion!
Robert L. Glass
Summer, 1989

A COLLECTION OF PITHY THOUGHTS FROM THIS BOOK

For the technical practitioner

The knowledge of practice sometimes exceeds that of theory. Because of that, theory sometimes proposes inappropriate solutions to practical problems. But when the knowledge of theory exceeds that of practice— and, inevitably, it will—it is important for practice to listen to what it has to say.

Some technologies with largely modest but nevertheless important potential benefit to software are reuse, prototyping, incremental development, 4GLs, CASE tools, and appropriately chosen metrics. We know the benefits are modest, in spite of claims to the contrary, because of (1) expert judgments from those who've been there and done that, and (2) emerging experimental results.

There is a missing link between methodological approaches to design and representational methods for writing design down. That missing link is creative or cognitive design, and it is the most important part of the design process.

Software error removal is difficult and rarely completely successful. However, with rigorous approaches to testing and cost-effective approaches to review we can build good software and believe in its reliability.

Software maintenance, for all the effort put into it, still seems to be poorly understood and appreciated by both management and academe. They call it a problem when in fact it is a solution, a service that we in software uniquely offer. They decouple the subjects of maintenance and quality when in fact they are intimately entwined. They fail to acknowledge one of the few true principles of software engineering, single-point control.

Software quality, for all the lip service we pay to it, tends to be under- achieved. Management and academe make its achievement a management issue even while acknowledging that only technologists know how to do it. They concentrate on measuring the measurable instead of quality itself. They are unaware of the best research in quality metrics, and as a result we dabble in quality metrics that have little intrinsic value.

User interfaces are one of the few true breakthroughs in the last decade.

While we pay attention to the excitement of bigger and better toolsets, we have not paid attention to the mundane need of software developers for a minimum standard toolset, the hammer, saw, and pliers of software.

Flexing software requirements are probaby the greatest plague on software technology. It's hard to shoot at a moving target.

Whatever happened to the fun in software? Does it go away with age, or discipline, or bureaucracy, or what? How many people trade in some of their success in order to have fun?

For the managment practictioner

The expectation of productivity and quality breakthroughs dulls the ability to appreciate and accept more modest methodological improvement. Furthermore, most such expectations are doomed to be dashed.

The biggest problems in software lie in poor management, not in poor technology.

Standards help us produce better software, but this is a case where less is probably more. Having too many standards leads to lack of enforcement and thus to lack of use.

Greatness is transient. The greats of the software past were coders, then researchers, then entrepreneurs. It is not obvious where the next generation of greatness will come from.

Everybody has been talking about productivity, but hardly anyone has really done anything about it.

Poor estimation is more responsible for the so-called "software crisis" than any other factor. We look for technology to solve problems that are in fact managerial.

Individual differences are the acknowledged key to software productivity and quality. The trouble is we don't know what to do about them.

For the researcher

In the early stages of a new discipline, one of the best ways of building theory is to examine good practice.

Far more breakthroughs are promised in research grant proposals and entrepreneurial training than are ever delivered. Those promises are either born of ignorance or poor ethics, and they tend to drown out more substantive, less exciting work.

COBOL may indeed be a very bad language, but all the others for its application domain are so much worse. Designing a better COBOL may be one of the most promising unexplored research issues of our time.

A large body of knowledge falls through the cracks of most literature searches. As a result, our research does not acknowledge some important work done on government-funded contracts, and by industry (e.g., vendors).

Our concern with substantiation through referencing the past may suppress publication of seminal ideas.

The research world and the practitioner world have largely broken off any meaningful communication. There is a desperate bidirectional need for bridge builders to span the gap.

Part of this gap is the lack of experimental research. Without an experimental component, computer science is not really science, and software engineering is not really engineering.

For the educator

Teaching design as methodology and representation is not enough. We now understand enough about the creative aspect of design to teach that, too.

Computer science scolds practice for lagging theory and then, when it comes time to teach new concepts like 4GLs and CASE tools, says it can't afford the cost.

The Software Engineering Institute has a slowly growing body of teaching materials essential to software engineering education. And, for the most part, they are free!

Software maintenance is simply not taught in most educational institutions. Educators don't understand that there is significant technical content to the topic.

Software engineering has been the place we tend to teach the much more universal topic of problem solving. The so-called "software life cycle," for example, is nothing more than the set of steps involved in solving *any* problem. Why isn't problem solving taught in the acedemic core curriculum?

Understanding the application domain is far more important than we have believed. Proper appreciation of domain differences may eventually lead us to domain-specific methodologies, tools, languages . . . and perhaps even education.

Appendix

Many of these essays were previously published, perhaps in one of my regular columns in *System Development* ("Software Reflections"), or the "Editor's Corner" of the *Journal of Systems and Software* or in *Software Magazine* ("Software Folklore"), or perhaps as a free-lance piece for *Computerworld* or *Datamation*.

The past history of these various essays is shown in the table below.

Essay	Previously Published In
An Overview of the Battleground	
• Which Comes First, Theory or Practice?	JSS, SD
• "Dangerous and Misleading"—A Look at Software Research via the Parnas Papers	SD, JSS
• "No Silver Bullet"—A Look at Software Research via the Fred Brooks Article	SD, JSS
• A Report From the Best and Brightest	—

Legend:

CUPS	*Confessions of a Used Program Salesman*, Will Tracz, to be published
CSM	*Proceedings of the 1989 Conference on Software Maintenance*
CW	*Computerworld*
D	*Datamation*
GCS	*Notices of the German Computer Society Technical Interest Group on Fault-Tolerant Computing Systems*
JSS	*Journal of Systems and Software*
SD	*System Development*
SESY	*Proceedings of the 1989 Italian Software Engineering Symposium*
SM	*Software Magazine* (formerly *Software News*)
SMN	*Software Maintenance News*
TT	*Proceedings of the 1987 Workshop on Software Technology Transfer*

Index